Oaxacan Ceramics

OAXACAN ceramics

Traditional Folk Art by Oaxacan Women

Lois Wasserspring

Photographs by Vicki Ragan

CHRONICLE BOOKS
SAN FRANCISCO

Text copyright © 2000 by Lois Wasserspring.
Photographs copyright © 2000 by Vicki Ragan.

Library of Congress Cataloging-in-Publication Data available.
ISBN 0-8118-2358-X

Designed by Michael Hentges
Typeset in Cochin with Pixie display
Printed in Hong Kong

Distributed in Canada by
Raincoast Books
8680 Cambie Street
Vancouver, British Columbia V6P 6M9

10 9 8 7 6 5 4 3 2 1

Chronicle Books
85 Second Street
San Francisco, California 94105

www.chroniclebooks.com

page 1: *Merman*, Josefina Aguilar
page 2: *Family of Flower Sellers*, Irene Aguilar

Collection Credits

We would like to thank the generosity of the following
collectors, galleries, and museums who graciously allowed
their ceramic works to be photographed for this book:

Colección Artesanías Cocijo, p. 25
Colección Corazón del Pueblo, pp. 26, 33, 91, 105, 106,
    123 top, 126
Cathe Dailey, p. 80 top right
William Goldman, p. 97
Vera Kandt, pp. 59, 99, 111
Ariel and Veronica Kaplan, pp. 27, 93, 95
Dr. Neal Kass, p. 44
Margaret Keys, p. 103
Colección La Mano Mágica, pp. 31, 88 top, 89
Mexican Fine Arts Center Museum, Chicago, pp. 24, 32, 98
Mexican Fine Arts Center Museum, gift of JoAnn and
    Cesáreo Moreno, p. 115 left figure
JoAnn and Cesáreo Moreno, p. 115 right figure
Jan Summer, pp. 68, 69, 113, 132
Sharon Watkins, pp. 50, 56, 90 bottom, 100

Contents

Dedication

A las valientes

artesanas oaxaqueñas:

Dolores Porras

Guillermina Aguilar

Josefina Aguilar

Irene Aguilar

Concepción Aguilar

Angélica Vásquez

Preface

This book began, without my knowing of it, a long time ago. I still treasure the two earthenware angels that my beloved *comadre*, Lini de Vries, gave me soon after I arrived in Mexico to begin thesis research. Doña Isaura Alcántara Díaz's soulful angels have stood guard on a sill in my kitchen since then, radiating a gentle spirituality over kitchen tables stacked, through the years, with lecture notes and academic papers, baby food, soccer cleats, and college applications. Long after I received this treasured gift, as if these guardian angels were somehow nudging me along, my research led me back to Doña Isaura's daughters.

My academic interests have long centered on the lives of Latin American women, and in the early nineties, I began a project on artisan women in Oaxaca, Mexico. Although Oaxaca is famous for its myriad of crafts, the most prominent female artisans, known throughout Mexico and beyond its borders, are all ceramists. I sought out each of these talented potters, and, with characteristic generosity, each spent dozens of hours helping me to understand more fully both her life and her art. Talking with these artisans over many years convinced me of the relevance of their stories—and their ceramics—for a larger audience. Hence this book. In it, I focus on the ceramic art of six renowned Oaxacan women. There are, of course, many other gifted artisans making other types of pottery in Oaxaca; I have made no attempt to be comprehensive here. This book is the story of these remarkable women and the splendid ceramics they create.

I am deeply grateful to some very special institutions and individuals whose generosity and support have allowed me to research and write this book. At various times, both Wellesley College and the Marion and Jasper Whiting Foundation have supported my fieldwork in Oaxaca financially. Wellesley College additionally gave me the research leave that allowed me the time to write. The David Rockefeller Center for Latin American Studies at Harvard University provided me with a wonderful space to work on my various writing projects, and the help of its superb staff.

As I have researched these artisan women's lives over the last several years, I have become indebted to a number of hard-working assistants, many of them my students. In the early stages of my research, the assistance in Oaxaca of Susan Hulick, Louisa Ollague, and Carolina Cruz allowed me to decide the direction of my focus on women artisans. I was ably helped in the task of transcribing and/or translating my mountain of taped interviews by Emi Kamura, Serena Cosgrove, Phil Pardi, Clara Marín, and María Colbert. Special thanks to Laura Waterbury for additional help translating when deadlines loomed. The energy, talent, and dedication of Sarah Lucas, my former student, who transcribed and/or translated many of my interviews that had been taped under less than ideal conditions, enabled me access to important materials.

My research in Oaxaca has always been enriched by the presence of some extraordinary people. I owe a great deal to the exceptional generosity of Mary Jane Gagnier de Mendoza, Rosa Blum Pérez, and Henry Wangeman. They, along with Enrique Audiffred, Ramón Fosada, and Vera Kandt, have unstintingly shared with me their knowledge and love of *arte popular*. Teodoro López Jiménez, José Luis Décaro, Nicodemus Bartolo Vásquez, Angela García Hernández, and Daniel Hernández Rodríguez spent valuable time helping me to understand the history of folk art commerce in Oaxaca. I want to thank each of them. Special thanks, too, to Gudrun Dohrmann, for the skill with which she helped me locate resources that I needed at the excellent library of the Instituto Welte, and to Jesús Froylan Llaguno León, *taxista extraordinario*, for helping me move through the valley to where I had to go.

My colleague at Wellesley, Lorraine Elena Roses, and my office mate at the Rockefeller Center, Juan Carlos Moreno Brid, have been both patient and generous with their answers to the many questions about fact and nuance that emerged as I prepared the final text. My membership in the Oxford Street Writing Group has been a delight; my writing has benefited from the group's serious and kindly criticism. I am grateful to Marcia Yudkin for her skilled editorial assistance.

Special friends have helped me through the various stages of my work—and my life—with loving encouragement and support. Martha Rees took the time to read drafts and offer insightful comments. Kathryn Kay, Gobi Stromberg, and Kathy Weingarten were there to listen or talk or read or laugh or hug when I needed them most. I love them all dearly.

I am blessed with two marvelous children, Sarah Natchez and Jonathan Natchez, and I want to thank them in print for all the warmth, high spirits, sense of adventure, and good-naturedness—traits clearly inherited from their wonderful father—with which they accompanied me on trips to Oaxaca all these years, even when they were too young to fully appreciate its magic.

Finally, to these remarkable women artisans of Oaxaca, who so graciously allowed me into their lives, I want to express my deepest gratitude. They have taught me a great deal about grace, about strength, and about creativity. I dedicate this book to them.

opposite:
La Virgen del Apocalipsis:
Virgin of the Apocalypse
Josefina Aguilar

Introduction

The bus ride due south from the provincial capital, Oaxaca de Juárez, to Ocotlán de Morelos takes only forty-five minutes, passing through some of the spectacular vistas for which Oaxaca—and Mexico—is justly famous. The rugged mountains in the distance, the domes of colonial churches glimpsed through verdant clusters of trees, the dozens of villages dotting the landscape—all contribute to the majesty of landscape that is Oaxaca.

At the entrance to Ocotlán, a sign—"Ocotlán: population 10,300"—announces that the community has shed its rustic status and can no longer be considered merely a village. Yet it is the flurry of activity immediately behind the sign that draws one's attention. An enormous tourist bus waits alongside a fence that has a wonderful array of ceramic figures piled jauntily along its brim. Inside, the courtyard is teeming with visitors admiring the colorful, fanciful forms created by Josefina Aguilar and her family. A table shielded from the sun to the left of the entrance holds the ceramic creations available for sale, and all epitomize the vibrant whimsy and charm that we have come to associate with Mexican folk art. Virgins and mermaids jostle for space with amorous skeleton couples embracing on park benches. Naughty *damas de la noche*—women of the night—cigarettes dangling from lipstick-stained mouths, strut behind stolid earthenware matrons peddling their wares—mangoes, watermelons, guavas. The profusion of colors is dazzling: pineapple-yellow crosses, ruby-red fish tails, emerald cloaks.

At the center of attention is Josefina herself, a proud, reserved woman of fifty-four, mother of nine, already grandmother to nine. She is accustomed to accolades, having been accorded many honors for almost three decades now for her artistry as a leading figural ceramist in Mexico. Her fame has long since spread beyond Mexico's borders to include international recognition. She was just a young girl when Nelson Rockefeller, an avid pioneer folk art collector, first arrived in the 1960s with an entourage and proceeded to buy up her store of work. His last visit, only months before he died in 1979, astonished her only because his purchases even denuded her fence: he insisted on taking with him every figure perched on its edge, albeit weather-worn and faded.

Josefina's older sister and next-door neighbor, Guillermina Aguilar, remembers Rockefeller's last visit with astonishment as well. "We were so poor then, so very poor. Our home here was then only two rooms, made of tin and cardboard. He bought *everything*, even the broken pieces!" Two decades later her amazement at this memory still reflects on her face. But now she too has adapted to the frequent attention of government officials, gallery owners, and tourists. Like her younger sister, Guillermina has exhibited her work internationally, and has even, on occasion,

opposite:
Market Woman
Concepción Aguilar

Unpainted Water Jugs
Guillermina Aguilar

acted as Mexico's "folk art ambassador" abroad. Her ceramic creations mirror the charm and brilliant coloration of Josefina's work, but have their own distinctive style. Her enchanting water jugs with humorous animal heads—beribboned donkeys, festive roosters, smirking cows—are her own innovation. Humor aside, Guillermina's deep religiosity leaves its mark on her creative output: nativities, Virgins, saints, and biblical scenes like the Last Supper crowd her workshop shelves, vibrant testimony to the depth of her faith.

Next door, Irene Aguilar, Josefina's and Guillermina's younger sister, extends the artistic tradition of this remarkable family of ceramists. Irene's dynamism is contagious. A small woman, she has long since discarded the traditional long braids favored by her older sisters for a more contemporary look. Her energy is palpable; her quick wit enchants her visitors as much as her talent in clay. She, too, has achieved renown for her painted ceramic figures and composite scenes—wonderful angels with wings spread wide, statuesque señoritas holding armloads of flowers and fruit, a procession of wedding guests celebrating a happy couple. Often a visiting artist at museums in the States, frequently a visitor to Santa Fe, New Mexico, where she gives demonstrations of her skills, Irene has seen her life unfold in ways unimaginable to the girl of her youth. That her craft could be the source of so much satisfaction in her life, let alone the fame, surprises her even now.

The fourth and youngest Aguilar sister, Concepción, completes the creative ensemble of these amazing siblings. More peripatetic than the others, she has only recently moved back to the highway locale near her sisters to take advantage of the tourist traffic. Slightly less well known than her siblings because she has come to work in clay full time only in the last decade, Concepción loves to make the figures of the great Mexican muralist, Diego Rivera, and his wife, Frida Kahlo, come alive in her hands. Peasant women bent with the weight of calla lilies share table space in her one-room home with Fridas, all with their distinctive brows, some with monkeys sitting on their shoulders, others with parrots or cats draped along their arms. All of her figures vibrate with intense Mexican colors: magenta, turquoise, scarlet, indigo.

✻   ✻   ✻

To reach Santa María Atzompa, a pottery-producing village four miles northwest of the state capital, a traveler must board a bus and return to Oaxaca de Juárez. On a Friday, traditional market day in Ocotlán, all the buses teem with people, turkeys, flowers, and mounded baskets wafting the rich scents of cilantro, cinnamon, and chilies. Hugging the western edge of the city, the bus to Atzompa will move at a snail's pace on a Friday because of the preparations already underway to prepare for Oaxaca's own fabled Saturday market, the largest in Mexico. Passing the crowded and bustling market area, amid the shouts and unloading, the bus soon crosses the Río Atoyac, once mighty it is claimed, but now reduced to a mere trickle. Heading in the direction of the majestic archaeological site of Monte Albán, the bus soon turns sharply to the right and heads down a dusty main road. Blue signs with the tourist icon for pottery announce the arrival in Santa María Atzompa.

Dolores Porras working

Here live two unusually talented women whose artistic prominence has been recognized both locally and abroad. On the road into the community, a new large, black sign points the way left to the home of "the pioneer" in colored pottery, Dolores Porras. Dolores is, in person, as imposing as her sign. Expansive in girth and personality, at sixty-two she has a generous nature mirrored in both her work in clay and her relationships. A doting grandmother (to twenty-three at last count!), she is not primarily a figural ceramist, but rather creates large planters, platters, vases, and candleholders with a distinctive fluidity of form and shape. Well known for her multicolored glazed ware, she and her husband helped invent the double-firing process that bakes her swirls of colored clay directly onto her pots while they are being fired. Chosen as the representative of the state of Oaxaca to several national artisan tours, she, too, often demonstrates her potting skills while exhibiting her ceramics in the United States.

From Dolores's home, past Atzompa's imposing colonial church, and straight uphill, one reaches the compound of the youngest star in this galaxy of female artisan luminaries in the valley of Oaxaca. Angélica Vásquez appears as frail as Dolores Porras is rotund, yet her diminutive stature conceals a formidable personality and a prodigious talent. She sculpts unglazed clay in natural colors into inventive and intricate compositions. Her terra-cotta figures tumble from conch shells and angels' wings. Her deft hands move quickly, as if they have a life of their own, forming minuscule fantastic creatures and Lilliputian people. All the while Angélica, never even glancing at her fingers, enchants visitors with her eloquent commentary on village life. Her work is increasingly sought after by collectors, and she has already had several solo exhibitions of her imaginative and fanciful ceramic creations.

❖   ❖   ❖

One of the poorest states in the Mexican republic, Oaxaca has limited agricultural production and few industries. A short and often irregular rainy season (June to October) makes it difficult to produce even the primary crops of the poor, maize and beans. The region lacks the factories that provide alternate employment for unskilled workers in the north of Mexico.

The difficulty of earning a living in Oaxaca comes across graphically in the landscape of the valley. As the road to Ocotlán begins to ascend a mountain ridge, it passes two neighborhoods of squatter settlements on either side of the road. Settled as "parachute" communities by peasants "landing" in the stealth of night to claim their plots of land, they are valuable because of their location next to the municipal garbage dump. In the opportunity-scarce economic environment of Oaxaca, picking resalable items from the garbage affords a living to many.

The official minimum wage in Oaxaca stands at around three dollars a day. Fully a quarter of all paid workers make less than that. Even the passage of national policies aimed at job creation, such as Mexico's signing of the North American Free Trade Agreement (NAFTA), have failed to produce beneficial effects in a state like Oaxaca, where businesses are loath to move because of poor roads, unreliable electricity, and weak communication systems. They prefer to locate in the industrialized north, thereby reinforcing the great economic divide in Mexico between its richer northern region and its impoverished south.

Oaxacans, both men and women, have the lowest life expectancy in the country. In contrast to other states in Mexico, Oaxaca experiences a regular net loss of population: Outmigration in search of economic opportunity elsewhere stands at one of the highest levels in the entire Republic. For Oaxacan women in particular, poverty strikes hard: The state's rates of both infant and maternal mortality soar above others in the nation. While the overall Mexican illiteracy rate for women is fifteen percent, thirty-five percent of Oaxacan women are illiterate. For the older generation, more than sixty percent of Oaxacan women over forty cannot read or write.

Oaxaca's opulent, lush culture offers a stark contrast to its economic poverty. Its abundance manifests itself architecturally, archaeologically, and in the unsurpassed human resources of its people. The magnificent colonial buildings, the imposing baroque facades of its monuments, and the exuberance and color stemming from its large indigenous population all serve to underscore the wealth that resides in Oaxaca, too.

In *arte popular*, the art that emerges from popular culture, Oaxaca's richness shows itself most fully. The legendary folk art traditions of Oaxaca include wondrous textiles, intricate basketweaving, fabled wood carvings, exquisite gossamer-fine jewelry echoing the designs of centuries, and skilled metal work ranging from jewel-toned tin soldiers to artistically etched machetes and knives. The weavings alone demonstrate the craft wizardry of Oaxacan hands in the bounty of *rebozos* (shawls), embroidered blouses, *sarapes*, woven belts, purses, and *huipiles* (the tunic-like garment worn by indigenous women).

Throughout the valley, villages continue to specialize in the production of particular crafts, just as many of them did over five hundred years ago before the arrival of the Spaniards. The wood carving villages of Arrazola, San Martín Tilcajete, and La Unión spill in different directions over the valley floor; Teotitlán del Valle continues to weave its serapes; Santo Tomás Jalieza weaves its belts; San Antonino conserves the tradition of its delicate floral embroidery. In fact, the visual cornucopia of folk art displayed everywhere in Oaxaca prompted some officials to argue that a regional popular art museum was not necessary there. "Oaxaca is a *living* folk art museum," they claimed.

As many as 400,000 of the state's three million inhabitants create folk art for sale. For the great majority of these craftspeople, artisan work serves as a means of supplementing the meager incomes gained from farming. Increasingly, however, craft production has become an important full-time economic occupation for many. Both the lack of other employment opportunities and the spiraling influx of tourists explain the renewed economic significance of artisan work. Tourism in particular,

La China Oaxaqueña:
Festival Dancer
Guillermina Aguilar

as the fastest-growing industry in Oaxaca, has reinforced artisan production, resulting in a virtual explosion of creativity and inventiveness. For its sheer quantity of distinguished crafts, as well as the immense variety of folk art that it produces, Oaxaca is unsurpassed in Mexico for the depth and breadth of its popular art.

The cultural richness reflected by its artisan work is seen most clearly in that most popular of folk arts, pottery. This is the most widely practiced craft in Oaxaca, indeed, in all of Mexico. More artisans work in this most elemental medium, the earth itself, than in any other craft throughout the Republic. This stems from the widespread use of clay pots at home in Mexican villages, coupled with the ceremonial and ritual importance of clay objects such as incense burners and candlesticks. The demand for either fine traditional utilitarian pieces or appealing, decorative clay objects by the new consumers who come from beyond a community's borders—national and international tourists—has fueled pottery production even more.

The variety of pottery available in Oaxaca is staggering. The most common type is finished in the natural color of the clay, although the diversity of earthenware alone is vast. Pieces can be simply shaped without further adornment, or the natural clay can be decoratively brushed or etched. More elaborate ceramic work may be polished, painted, or glazed, the colored glazing technique a sixteenth-century Spanish colonial innovation unknown by the potters of Mexico's great Indian civilizations. Often, the design, shape, or color of the ceramic piece immediately signals its place of origin, village by village.

Guillermina Aguilar, a natural-born teacher, classifies clay work in the valley of Oaxaca as "always black, green, or red." She is referring to the famous black pottery of San Bartolo Coyotepec, down the road from Ocotlán: The celebrated color comes from smoking the pieces during the firing process. Green identifies the major type of lustrous pottery for which Santa María Atzompa is known. Although Dolores Porras and Angélica Vásquez apprenticed, like everyone else in their village, in the production of this gleaming, emerald-green glazed ware, both women have developed their signature styles by drawing upon other ceramic roots in their community.

Guillermina's category of red clay covers the broadest range of ceramics in the Oaxaca valley. It includes the Aguilar sisters' painted creations, which are first formed and fired and only then painted. It also includes the russet and nutmeg-hued unpainted compositions of Angélica, who achieves multitonality in her work by the use of two different shades of clay or, occasionally, by her application of a slip—clay diluted to a wash—to parts of her design. And it encompasses the multicolored, glazed pottery of Dolores, whose use of pigment in the firing process requires a second "cooking" of her ware.

Oaxacan pottery is essentially a woman's art. The overwhelming majority of craftspeople who work in clay are women. In a few Oaxacan communities such as Atzompa and Coyotepec, men occasionally work as ceramists; in some historically distinctive areas, such as the Isthmus of Tehuantepec, men alone work in clay. But in general, pottery is made by women, raising some interesting questions about being female in Mexico.

Wind, Water, and Light
Angélica Vásquez

Why is it, for example, that pottery garners the lowest prices of all the major crafts in Mexico? Given the laboriousness of production—from digging for the clay, preparing it for use, shaping the piece, drying it, and firing it in the kiln, with all the risks of breakage inherent in the firing process—it is remarkable that ceramic pieces are sold for so little. While it is true that most artisans in Mexico make only a precarious living from their craft, the gap between effort and reward is probably the greatest in ceramic work. One wonders if there is not a gender connection here. The woodcarvers of the Oaxaca valley, predominantly men, get substantially higher prices for their animal figures than virtually any of the female ceramists working in the area. The use of the machete by the male woodcarvers somehow elevates their craft to the category of "sculpture," while the very mundane origins of clay production, stemming from family use in the home, diminishes its value.

In fact, it is not just in the craft world of clay that women's artisan efforts take a back seat. In all branches of artisan work, women's contributions are often hidden or devalued. Although artisans are frequently anonymous and invisible—the creators of baskets or textiles come immediately to mind—the creative efforts of women in particular tend to be slighted. The men of San Martín Tilcajete, Arrazola, and La Unión sign their names on their wonderful wooden creatures. But after

carving the animals, they hand them over to their wives and daughters to painstak-
ingly transform the bare wood into the vibrantly colored, decorated forms that
attract buyers. Throughout the artisan world, when females paint or polish or construct, their efforts are simply considered a normal part of family responsibilities.
Along with this expectation of women's natural assistance comes an assumption that
their creative endeavors do not require acknowledgment or pay.

These ideas about women's inherent family obligations may account for the
strange data about women's economic activity found in the official Oaxaca census.
Eighty-eight percent of Oaxacan women over the age of twelve, we are told, are
"economically inactive." One needs to spend only a few hours meandering through
any village in the Oaxaca valley to understand the important economic contributions
of women. Women are hauling water; they are gathering firewood; they are tending
animals. They are weaving, potting, and making baskets. They are selling the herbs
they have grown and the food they have just cooked. But women's labor within the
family compound, even if it is virtually full-time artisan work, is not perceived as real
work. Not only the census takers, but often the women themselves see this work as
part of their roles as dutiful wives and daughters. Of those women who are catego-
rized officially as economically active, more than forty percent receive less than the
minimum wage. For artisan women who seek income outside of their homes, it
means, at best, working in the lower-paying crafts and always for the lowest wages.

Oaxacan artisan women are, therefore, clearly affected by the fundamental
ideas about women—and men—in Mexican life. Simply saying, however, that
Oaxaca, like virtually all of Mexico, is a man's world overlooks important nuances.
Machismo prevails, certainly; to be manly is to be aggressive, authoritative, domi-
neering. The virile male is one who claims his prerogatives and asserts his right to
dominion. The ideal woman also conforms to stereotype: She is the devoted wife and
nurturing mother who makes marriage and motherhood the core of her existence.

Yet here an added factor is the flip side of the *machismo* coin, *marianismo*: the
cult of the Virgin Mary. A good woman mirrors Mary in the depth of her patience
and self-sacrifice. Like Mary, she attains saintliness in her devotion to her children
and in deferring to and obeying men. And like Mary, she has great spirituality and
an unwavering moral compass. One consequence of infusing women with the nobil-
ity of the Virgin Mother is the extraordinary respect accorded women throughout
Mexico. Particularly in their roles as mothers, women are placed on pedestals of
reverence and esteem.

But pedestals can be peculiarly unstable places to perch. For one, they tip
easily. The good woman, devoted to home and hearth, can quickly become, if she

ventures outside alone, the "bad woman" of the street. The divide between *casa* (home) and *calle* (street) remains, even today, a cultural chasm that a respectable woman often dares not cross, particularly in more rural states like Oaxaca. And while mothers are glorified, men continue to assert their right to command and rule. The veneration of women can ironically confirm the authority of men. The good woman is still the female who submits and obeys.

❖   ❖   ❖

Within these economic and cultural realities, the success of these celebrated women artisans is all the more remarkable. Ranging in age from forty-one to sixty-two, these six women have developed regional, national, and international reputations as major contemporary folk artists. Their ceramic art can be found in museums, galleries, and private collections in Mexico and around the world. Already counted among the most distinguished of Mexican artisans, their honors continue to accumulate year by year. Quite in contrast to the more typical expectation of female invisibility, these women are increasingly visible—and prominent. Their careers are on a roll.

The Aguilar sisters—Guillermina, Josefina, Irene, and Concepción—received honors as an entire family of distinguished artisans in a special exhibition of the work of all the siblings at the new folk art museum located in San Bartolo Coyotepec, Oaxaca, in the spring of 1997. The sisters' work was again chosen for tribute in an exposition in the United States in 1998 at Chicago's Mexican Fine Arts Center Museum. The state government recently singled out Dolores Porras for special public praise for her enrichment of Oaxacan culture. Angélica Vásquez has won, among a host of other recent honors, four prestigious first-place awards in state and national artisan competitions in the past year, including an impressive award from a national cultural foundation for innovation in ceramics. ARIPO, the official state artisan organization, recently selected her and Irene Aguilar for solo exhibitions. In 1999, Irene Aguilar won an important national award for the distinguished course of her entire career in ceramics.

These exceptional women have triumphed through long years of hard work, and at times, profound personal struggle. Like the inherent vitality of the art they produce, their life stories reflect indomitable spirits and inspiring strength. All of their lives have been deeply affected by being female, yet they have been able to use personal grit, the sustenance of family, and the resources of their communities to expand their opportunities despite economic and cultural constraints. In fact, family and community roots propelled each of these women artisans to the magic of working with clay.

The four Aguilar sisters at the wedding of Concepción's daughter, Estela. Clockwise from top left: **Irene, Concepción, Josefina, and Guillermina**

Ocotlán de Morelos

Ocotlán de Morelos, the home of the Aguilar sisters, is in many ways a typical rural Oaxacan town, with the unlikely distinction of being one of the few communities in Oaxaca not studied by the hordes of anthropologists who have descended upon the valley. This is no doubt due to Ocotlán being basically a *mestizo* town (of mixed Spanish and Indian heritage), and while touched, like everything in Oaxaca, by the richness of pre-Hispanic traditions, it is not steeped in indigenous custom, dress, or language. Tourists come for the excitement of the Friday market, and more recently, because of the growing international fame of contemporary painter Rodolfo Morales, whose gratitude to his home community is shown in his generous restoration of historic buildings and his enchanting murals inside the town hall.

But Mexican guidebooks also denote Ocotlán as a major pottery center, although very few of its inhabitants work in clay. In fact, the town's reputation for ceramics stems primarily from the clay creations of just the Aguilar sisters, and ultimately, from the inventive imagination of their remarkable mother, Doña Isaura Alcántara Díaz.

Born in 1924, Doña Isaura struggled most of her life to eke out a living. After marrying Jesús Aguilar Revilla and giving birth to eight children—five daughters and three sons—she began to work in clay, discovering that she could earn some money by making and selling the inexpensive home-use pottery needed by all housewives in town. Sometimes working with a small group of other women from Ocotlán, Doña Isaura would produce her bowls of unglazed, natural-colored clay to sell at the weekly market. Her specialty soon became the traditional *apaxtle*, the most versatile of home pots—a round, flat-bottomed, thick-sided dish resembling a basin—especially favored for its varied domestic use by people in the area. She also became known for her *braseros*, shallow clay incense burners on tripod legs, used on altars, especially during the celebration of the Day of the Dead. With her creation of these important religious objects, Isaura became a true folk artisan, creating popular art directly linked to her community's social and ceremonial needs.

Isaura's creative genius came with the idea that she could use the medium of clay that she loved to create totally new forms. She was particularly intrigued by the idea of sculpting in clay the rich human scene she saw unfold on a weekly basis in the market. In the very ordinary activity of the market scene in front of her, she saw potential splendor in clay. Vendors with their heads piled high with baskets of food, market women with carefully arranged produce and flowers, peasant women with full, long skirts and ribbons in their hair—all became the creative inspiration for innovation. She slowly experimented and expanded her repertory of ceramic figures, always stimulated by her immediate daily world. She created groupings of

opposite:

Candlestick Holders
Guillermina Aguilar

multiple figures, tableaux of daily life: baptisms, weddings, funerals. Her fertile imagination was constantly in motion: the traditional incense burner could perhaps become a fruit bowl if its legs were thickened and fanciful fish or lush flowers were mounted along its rim. As she honed her figural modeling skills, Isaura turned to the challenge of infusing feelings into her ceramic forms. She produced a range of evocative clay images: a mourning woman, huddled gracefully in her *rebozo*, tears rolling down her cheeks; a solemn angel, weighted down by the suffering of mortals. Ultimately, Isaura's ability to impart into the plasticity of clay the intensity of human emotion—the sadness, the grief, and the elation of human experience—represented her special gift.

With her innovative ceramics, Doña Isaura had moved from the realm of creating objects for domestic, ritual, or ceremonial use to decorative art. Her wonderful figures did not fit the mold of utilitarian folk craft: they had no use in the daily lives of Ocotlán's citizens. Her ceramic pieces were merely ornamental. Isaura Alcántara was really expanding the idea of popular art by taking it in a new direction. Her folk art became a celebration of culture itself. Her creations exude their cultural roots, and honor every aspect of it, from food to dress to custom and myth.

Discerning folk art enthusiasts did not take long to discover Isaura's charming figures. Alexander Girard, Nelson Rockefeller, and other high-profile collectors came to buy her wares. But Doña Isaura, like most women of her generation, was illiterate. She couldn't read or write, or even sign her name. Her husband, Jesús, an astute businessman, therefore signed his own name to her pieces. He, after all, had the communication skills to deal with buyers and expand sales. With this rationale, and the flourish of a cactus spine to etch his name, Jesús Aguilar became the celebrated artisan of Ocotlán.

And he achieved fame not only for the production of enchanting ceramic figures, but also, supposedly, for nurturing through his careful instruction the emerging ceramic talents of his offspring. Jesús did indeed help his wife with her clay creations, primarily by painting the figures after they were fired. At times, he even crafted some simpler shapes of clay himself, mainly the ceramic bells with whimsical animal heads for which the Aguilar family became known. But he neither created in his imagination nor constructed in his hands the clay compositions that collectors and tourists sought. For years, Jesús' artisan reputation continued, but eventually awareness spread that he had not really created these pieces, and museums scrambled to correct their error of attribution. Usually, given the confusion, they relabeled the pieces with a general credit to "the Aguilar family." In actuality, most of these early works were the clay creations of this one meticulous, passionate, and creative woman, whose authorship and talent were never acknowledged in her lifetime.

In a true sense, then, Doña Isaura's legacy is indeed in her daughters' hands. All of them feel an intense gratitude and an overwhelming sense of debt to her because of the creative inheritance she bequeathed to each of them. All the sisters acknowledge their own artisan roots in their mother's work. As children they watched, imitated, and learned from their mother, first about the general techniques of working with clay as she taught them to make *apaxtles*, and then about the art of giving free rein to imagination in crafting figures and tableaux.

Doña Isaura bequeathed them not only experience and instruction, but also, on a practical level, important connections which her talent had forged for the family with the shop owners, international collectors, and Mexican folk art experts who would eventually help her daughters develop their own careers. She gave them the option of learning a craft that could sustain them, an opportunity that these women now extend to their own children.

Guardian Angels
Doña Isaura Alcántara Díaz

Isaura died in 1968, only forty-four years old. Guillermina was twenty-six at the time, Josefina twenty-three, Irene seventeen, and Concepción only ten. Jesús, distraught and increasingly unstable after his wife's death, died eight years later in 1976. As with many families, the death of their parents became a turning point, and each daughter began to construct her own independent life. As they married and had children, they all took with them their mother's creative bequest. Today, they like to think of themselves as separate and distinct families of artisans, rather than one general Aguilar clan.

It was Josefina who was the first to realize the advantage of locating on the main road into town, because of the tourist traffic that usually streams into Ocotlán for the Friday market. Her sisters soon followed suit. For years, the Aguilar mantle rested on the shoulders of the three older sisters. The youngest sister, Concepción, has always worked in clay, but her personal circumstances made it necessary for her to work for her sisters, rather than strike out on her own. Only in the last decade has she established her own separate presence at the entrance to town. (A fifth sibling, brother Jesús, has very recently begun to work in clay after many other careers.) All of the Aguilars' inventive clay designs continue to reflect the immense power of Doña Isaura's original vision. Together, mother and daughters have created a popular art tradition that is part of the national folk art landscape, radiating a warmth that is quintessentially Mexican.

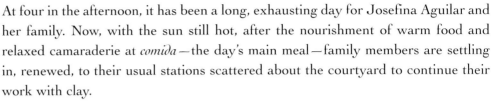

Josefina Aguilar

Josefina Aguilar

Funeral Procession
Josefina Aguilar

At four in the afternoon, it has been a long, exhausting day for Josefina Aguilar and her family. Now, with the sun still hot, after the nourishment of warm food and relaxed camaraderie at *comida* — the day's main meal — family members are settling in, renewed, to their usual stations scattered about the courtyard to continue their work with clay.

The day began at five in the morning when Josefina's husband, José, and five of their sons went three kilometers down the road to dig for more clay. For this strenuous work, the more muscle the better. The land where the few potters in town always got their clay now belongs to Josefina and her husband, who feel real satisfaction that they were able to buy it from the old man who owned it all those years before he died. They no longer have to pay each week for the clay they need.

On the other hand, getting to the clay is more difficult and dangerous than it might seem. The really good clay sits way down deep, ten feet, maybe even fifteen feet below the surface. You need luck to hit the right vein and strength to dig through dirt, rock, and sand until you do. During the rainy season, it is just too risky to even try. The walls of the trenches you must dig to reach the clay can collapse on you in a flash. The last time the family tried to get some clay out after the rains began, they almost had a tragedy. Two of the boys were way down below when everything started to come down on them: dirt, stones, and then, a really big rock. If they hadn't yelled for the rest of the family to pull them out quickly, they would have been crushed. So the pressure is on to load up on clay in May, before the rains usually come.

By nine in the morning, Josefina had shown up with Leticia, her only daughter, and one of her daughters-in-law with food for the men at work. It had meant a lot of late-night work for her yesterday preparing the *frijoles*, but she had to make sure the food would be ready. After all that hard work, the men would have scolded them if they were late. After eating, the men had continued digging for another five hours, but then they had to call it a day. Despite continuous shoveling, they kept hitting only dirt and sand. Then they had to scramble out of the way of a dangerous snake. Usually they aim for fifteen or sixteen sacks of clay; today nine hours of work resulted in much less. Still, they were grateful for what they did get, and felt their family had been blessed. They used to have to cart the clay along the road in a wheelbarrow, load by load. Now they had a pickup to do the job.

The greatest gift, though, had been given by the blessed Virgin of Juquila, whom they had all asked for help. When they bought the land with clay years before, there was no easy way to enter it. Another piece of land sat in front of it, and they always had to ask permission to get to their own. Worse, they had to cross a small ravine near the entrance. Most of the time the water at the bottom was only a trickle. But when the rains came, it became a torrent. They would have to wade across one by one, the water up to their knees. They'd asked the Virgin to help them have a safe way to get to their land, and their wish was granted. The owner of the land they had to cross suddenly decided to sell them a little piece five meters wide, enough for José to build a bridge. These days even their pickup could get in there to get the clay.

Family Altar for Day of the Dead
Josefina Aguilar

Now back at the family compound, as they position themselves to work, the turquoise paint on the wall behind them and the medley of vibrant colors on the nearby table of items for sale add an aura of electric energy to the scene, even though the workday has already been long and hard. Josefina is at her usual place, in a corner of the shaded patio on the left side of the courtyard. As always, she sits, like her mother and her grandmother before her, directly on the cold floor, legs doubled up under her. An *apaxtle* filled with water is close by, ready if she needs to moisten the clay. Holding a maguey thorn, she begins to etch the lines of a face in the elaborate figure of a market woman that she is molding. Clay fruits of every description—pineapples, plantains, mangoes, grapes—are next to her, ready to be pinched expertly onto the basket on the seller's head. Her granddaughter Josefinita is watching intently, mesmerized by her grandmother's quickly moving hands. One sees in the eight-year-old's gaze another link in the making in this generational chain of women who work in clay.

José García Cruz, Josefina's husband, is at his usual spot, to Josefina's left, carefully painting already-fired work. Between them is the special place left for their daughter, Leti, symbolically positioned at her mother's knee. Across the patio, facing the brilliant blue-green wall, Demetrio, now Josefina's eldest, focuses on mixing the unusual smokey colors he prefers for his own very popular work. His wife Arcenia faces him, absorbed, like José, in painting the clay pieces removed yesterday from the kiln.

As the other grandchildren return home from school, the bustle in the courtyard mounts. Very quickly a beehive of activity surrounds those concentrating on clay. Josefina's seventy-six-year-old mother-in-law, Estéfana Cruz Méndez, washes the afternoon dishes, helped by two of the wives of Josefina's other sons. Another daughter-in-law busies herself with laundry. Son Sergio, nineteen, begins his weekly task, kneading clay that has already been dried, pulverized, and mixed with water. He does this with his feet, as if mashing grapes to make wine. His "dance" on the clay can take him four or five hours until all the water is absorbed and the clay is ready to use. Amidst all the activity are the shouts and laughter from the children running about, and the quieter buzz of conversation from the adults.

Josefina's home bursts, like a ripe watermelon, with the vitality and zest of her family life. Her identity as a mother has dominated her life even more than her devotion to clay. She gave birth to her first child, Mario, when she was twenty-one; she delivered her last, Fernando, when she was thirty-eight. Between these two, she had six more sons and one daughter. Now, with four sons married, all of her daughters-in-law and grandchildren live with her as well. In part, this living arrangement

opposite:

Selling to the Faithful

Josefina Aguilar

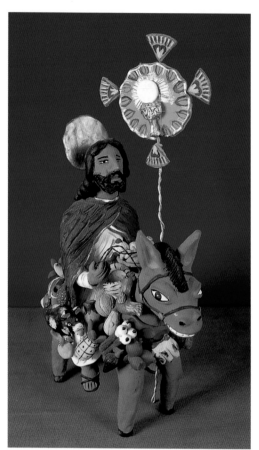

San Salvador
Josefina Aguilar

follows the custom of the region. It is Oaxacan practice that, after marriage, young couples live with the family of the groom. But in Josefina's case, there is also the magnet of clay. Her family is poised like an army mobilized to help. Only Martín, twenty-three, who has gravitated more to computers than to clay, and Fernando, fifteen, the youngest and still in school, do not take part in helping their mother create her popular art.

Josefina Aguilar's career as a craftsperson has enhanced, rather than detracted from, her role as a mother. As an artisan who has worked within her home, rather than outside of it, she has been able to continue to embody Mexican ideas of the good woman, despite her illustrious career. But she has also not escaped knowing the depths of a mother's pain. In 1993, her eldest son, Mario, by then a policeman with both state and federal rank, was murdered in a drug bust gone bad. He was only twenty-seven. "My son was doing us the favor of cleaning up the people who sell drugs, and they killed him," she says.

As a Mexican folk artist, fame came earlier to Josefina than it did to her sisters. Married to José and working in clay on her own even before her mother's death, her skill began to be noticed while she was in her early twenties. Photographs of her work soon began to appear in folk art publications; the publicity that came from winning a major Mexican award for ceramics in 1975 accelerated the process of recognition. As Mexican folk art began to be appreciated more widely within Mexico and worldwide, a number of books celebrating its charm were published in the late 1970s. In most of them, Josefina had arrived as a star. Her distinctive figures, somewhat like her mother's but with even more pronounced Zapotec profiles, and her *juegos*, multifigured scenes of Mexican life, received prominent billing along with the work of only a handful of other Mexican popular artists. Usually she and the famous ceramist Teodora Blanco, two decades her senior, were the sole women so honored. By the 1980s, European articles were published on her work; in 1985 she and José made their first trip outside of Mexico, to the United States, to exhibit her pieces. Since then she has received a steady stream of interest, awards, and publicity in recognition of her stature as a major Mexican figural ceramist.

Both Josefina and José still remember the fear and determination they felt when they decided, almost three decades ago, to locate at the entrance to Ocotlán. "We already had five children. When we came to live here, to rent, the owner told us, 'I'll give you a year; either you buy the place or you move out.' So we said to ourselves, we are going to work late, we are going to get up early, we may go without eating, but we are going to buy this place. That's how we did it." José would take a table out front on Fridays. "When the tourist buses came to the market on Fridays, they started to get off to see, and we started to sell and sell." Even with these sales, making ends meet was not easy. "Our house was only cardboard siding and sheet metal. Our kids went barefoot. Our fence was just bamboo." But hard work, and the desire, as Josefina puts it, "to move up" pushed them on. "That is the way it was for me, work on Sundays, on holidays, and sometimes I didn't sleep or eat, so that I could work."

Life is easier for them now. With the help of their children, now all grown, the really exhausting work—the digging, the kneading, the firing, the painting, the delivering—can be shared. The help of her daughters-in-law has meant that Josefina alone is not responsible for all the cooking, cleaning, washing, and ironing. Yet even now, after all the recognition and fame, all the many years of work, it is sometimes hard going. The expense of maintaining their family army is high. With twenty-five mouths to feed each day, they use nine pounds of *maíz* each morning just for their tortillas!

Fruit Bowl
Josefina Aguilar

But the progress of their lives also brings great satisfaction. They take pleasure in the material improvements they have been able to make: the new second floor, to welcome their sons' wives; the washing machine, where less than a decade ago stood a corral with six goats. For Josefina, the deepest satisfaction comes from her work. "I have liked my work a lot and I have tried to do it well. Sometimes people come here and they ask me to do a demonstration. I do it and they applaud, they talk, they chat, and then they say, 'Thank you very much, Señora,' and they touch my back and they say that it is all very lovely and I feel . . . How can I express it? . . . I feel so happy that they like my work."

Guillermina Aguilar

The altar in Guillermina Aguilar's home looks especially beautiful today. There are always flowers on it, but today a profusion of deep red roses spill out of glasses and jars both on the altar and on the floor in front. An old peasant woman had stopped by this morning, as she sometimes does, to sell her flowers, and Guillermina had felt moved to buy a lot. She puts flowers on her altar every day; a candle burns continuously, like those flickering now, in homage to her mother, whose altar resembled hers. It makes her feel that her mother is still with her, still transmitting her beliefs and wisdom.

Grandmother Clotilde
Guillermina Aguilar

Guillermina's altar takes up a corner of the large room that is the main living and work space for her family. With a dirt floor and dim light, the space exudes a dark, almost mysterious mood. At the far end of the room is the *horno*, the oven or kiln, where the clay figures are fired. A few feet in front is the kitchen area, centered around a fire with a traditional clay griddle or *comal*. Guillermina always works on a low stool, back to the wall, to the left of the entrance to the room. Her husband of thirty-seven years, Leopoldo García Cruz, sits next to her, today forming flattened clay into small bells.

At a long narrow table facing them both, five of their nine children are busy working, painting final details on the figures that each has begun to specialize in. Isabel, thirty-two, is carefully dabbing speckles of gold paint into the dramatic black cloak of a small *Virgen de la Soledad*. Juan, twenty-six, is applying a delicate tint of pink to the dome of an elaborate church. Silvia, twenty-five, has lined up several small mermaids and is brushing their scales in electric shades of red and blue. Fidel, twenty-nine, lifts one of the Apostles from his chair at a Last Supper he has fashioned out of clay and begins to blacken his beard. The youngest child, Polo, now twenty, has arranged a group of tiny clay images of Frida Kahlo and sits absorbed in coloring them in dazzling hues.

Guillermina herself is painting the figure of a woman in old-fashioned dress, styled from memories of the clothes of her grandmother Clotilde, her father's mother, a healer who cured people of fright. She has finished everything except the woman's ruffled scarf, which she will paint a bright red. All the same, Guillermina had hoped to have the piece finished by now, even though she knows that it always takes longer to paint her pieces than to shape them in the first place. But she had been interrupted by the municipal inspector, who came to check that they were not using freshly cut, green wood to fire their kiln. He had left, satisfied, as always, that they were following the new tree-protecting rules. In the mood of quiet concentration that fills the room, she can finish quickly now. The only sounds are soothing: the scratchings of her five new ducklings as they scurry beneath the altar, and the swish of the makeshift swinging cradle holding Isabel's daughter, Rosario, her thirteenth and most recent grandchild.

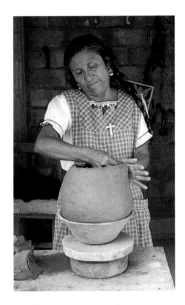

Guillermina Aguilar

When she is finally done, Guillermina decides to move outside to begin a new project in the warm sun. Like the rest of her family, she is delighted with the simple new entranceway they have constructed from the plain dirt passage that existed before. Now there is demonstration space and a work area on one side of the narrow walkway, and a *bodega*, with shelves displaying their ware, on the other. The changes make it easier for the tourists who come to buy; and now family members can work in good light and fresh air. As Guillermina walks the few paces to this new

Water Jug
Guillermina Aguilar

work space, she limps. When she fell in the street a while back, her husband took her immediately to a nearby community to see the local *huesero*, the traditional bone doctor. But he advised her to go to Oaxaca and have a modern doctor make her a cast. As an artisan, she had no social security, and with the wait at government clinics as long as three weeks, the family had to weather the cost of a private doctor. Even that expense could not produce a leg as good as before. Still, she says her leg feels fine when she has the opportunity to stretch it, like now. Arriving at the table outside, she reaches for some fresh clay.

Standing, she begins the process of making one of the large water jugs for which she is known. She will first form the base, and later invent a playful animal head for its spout. As she mounds the clay in front of her, she grabs a simple, improvised turntable consisting of two thick round disks, the top circle of wood, the bottom of stone, joined together with metal screws. Her husband made this crude lazy Susan for her; it would not be considered a real potter's wheel. Guillermina uses it only when a turning motion makes it easier to quickly produce a uniform shape to a large vessel she is forming. Virtually everything else she makes, particularly her figures, are molded, unassisted, by hand. She works the clay, her left hand rapidly spinning the turntable around while the fingers of her right hand pry

Bells and Incense Burner
Guillermina Aguilar

thick, loosely formed strips of clay from the mound and press them one by one to the clay base.

As she continues to use these long, fat ropes of clay to build up the sides of the jug, the rest of her children arrive. Her oldest daughter, Maximina, brings in little buckets of eggs, cheese, and squash from the rich plot of land she and her husband till not far away. Alejandro, at thirty-seven the eldest child, arrives soon after. He joins his father, who has come outside to start painting the animal faces of already-fired jugs. Julian, thirty-one, whose own career in clay has been boosted by a spate of recent awards, rushes in, also intending to help. Only daughter Lupe, recently married, has not yet arrived, but she too will come. All the children come every day to share the workload when there are orders to fill.

Since it is almost mealtime, Guillermina's daughters Silvia and Isabel begin to prepare the food. As the pungent smells of chilies, tomatoes, and onions fill the air, Leopoldo gently nudges Guillermina to stop working. But she shakes her head no. If she doesn't finish the jug now, the clay will dry up and she won't be able to work it any more. As the family gathers to sit down and eat without her, Guillermina manages to make everyone laugh. "This clay is very, very jealous," she says, smiling. "Imagine! It is more jealous than my husband, because my husband will wait for me, but the clay will not."

At fifty-seven, Guillermina is the eldest of the eight Aguilar siblings, and the one most tied to the rich customs of the past. Her appearance reflects her deep respect for traditional ways: Her hair is always done neatly in braids; her apron and shawl, symbols of a woman's decency, are part of her daily dress. More than her sisters, she has organized her household in tune with the habits of her youth. While her family owns a blender, she prefers not to use it, feeling that the machine ruins the good flavor of food. She and her daughters use the traditional grinding stone, the *metate*, to make savory *amarillo* or *verde* sauces, to grind the coffee beans they toast themselves, or the cacao beans they mix with cinnamon and sugar for hot chocolate. They have not yet cared to value speed—or ease—over the practices of the past.

Soft-spoken, with a wise manner, Guillermina radiates the *marianista* ideal. Like the big metal cross that hangs proudly from her neck, religion looms large in her life. Her deep Catholic faith has always anchored her, and it continues to sustain her during difficult times. She has come to believe that suffering is not to be avoided in this life; that it is, in fact, an opportunity for spiritual growth. Her religious commitment nourishes and comforts her, but it also protects. Mainly through her grandmothers, Guillermina learned of the various spirits from beyond that one could encounter in this world, such as *nahuales*—people who are no longer with us, but who can return in the form of magical animals with the power to either protect or do harm. For her grandparents, these spirits could be placated by special offerings. To protect their harvest, for example, they would leave four cigarettes, four glasses of *mezcal*, and four drops of blood around the perimeter of their land. For Guillermina, Catholic faith provides the protective shield. "I always tell my children," she says, "there are those things in life we do not want to believe in, but they are there." Thinking about God in those moments removes any danger. "'Look children,' I say, 'when you go to the fields, when you sense something—because the body can tell that which is not of this world—cross yourselves. Pray so that you will be protected, so that Our Father notices that you are remembering him.'"

Carrying Water
Guillermina Aguilar

Guillermina's commitment to traditional ways has enriched her life a great deal, but there are aspects of tradition that have made her very vulnerable. As a daughter, she was needed at home to help her mother with household chores, and therefore, never attended school. Like her sisters, she cannot read or write. "Sometimes when I go out," Guillermina notes, "I have to take one of the children

along so that they can tell me prices, or the name of a street." Without the skills of schooling, ceramists like Guillermina have to contend with more than the creative challenge of working with clay. To meet these difficulties, work and family become closely linked.

Guillermina's career as a folk artist began later than her sister Josefina's. The first Aguilar sibling to marry, she and her husband, Leopoldo (whose younger brother later became Josefina's husband), tried their hands at everything they could think of to establish their independence. Guillermina continued to make and sell *apaxtles*, as she had done in her mother's home. The young couple would hustle to Oaxaca before dawn to buy baked rolls not available in Ocotlán, returning by 6 A.M. to sell them. They would scramble on the weekends to Atzompa, a three-hour trip, to buy and then resell its marketable green pottery at home. At one point, Guillermina also cooked in a tiny restaurant; at another, she sold fruit. But by the time of her mother's death in 1968, with four children already to support, she knew that kind of hustling would never be enough, given the poverty of the Oaxacan countryside. "I said to my husband, 'Look, I am going to work in clay.' I knew that if I didn't, I wouldn't survive."

She began simply, making the traditional *braseros*, or incense burners, favored in her community for use on the Day of the Dead, and the ceramic bells with animal heads that her mother had designed at the suggestion of a Oaxacan folk art enthusiast. The *braseros* still hold a special place in her heart, connecting her, in their creation, to her mother and to her religious faith. She takes great pride in making them in the style of the past, with silhouettes encircling the rim of the shallow cup representing the souls of the dead, which are then painted in symbolic colors: white signifying the purity of the souls; blue, the ardor of faith; and black, the deep sadness of loss.

Quietly and steadily her reputation developed. One day in the early 1970s, a man from the nearby village of San Martín who had just been appointed Oaxaca's representative for FONART, the government agency supporting folk crafts, came to see her. It was an important moment: "You're Guillermina; well, we need work. But I don't want the things you are making. What I want are skeletons. Here's money, and you pay it back with skeletons." He wanted dressed skeleton figures and colorful candlesticks in the shape of skulls, popular Mexican motifs, especially for the Day of the Dead. She could not believe her good fortune, but at the same time, doubted that she was up to the task. Her husband convinced her she was. The ceramic figures she began producing very quickly revealed her special abilities.

opposite:
Apaxtle:
traditional water basin
Guillermina Aguilar

With her confidence fortified, her imagination unleashed, and her talent established, Guillermina's career as a prominent ceramist took off. An invitation to meet the Queen of Spain soon followed (a thrilling but embarrassing experience: "I was very pregnant with Juan and I had to get up to greet the Queen. I had my huge stomach. How could I hide it?"). Another invitation came immediately after that to exhibit in the United States. The opportunities, awards, and honors have continued ever since. Yet in her devout and self-effacing manner, Guillermina will not acknowledge her own part in her success: "Thank God, with God's strength, we came out ahead."

Her accomplishments, however, have not entirely eliminated the scrambling to stay afloat that she and Leopoldo endured in their younger years. Working with clay is not an easy way to make a living. When there are orders, the workday is grueling—"whatever the body will take"—to finish what has been promised. But the market in folk art, like any other market, has its ups and downs. When there are no orders, Guillermina and her family must fall back on the typical survival strategies of generations of Mexican rural folk: land and animals. They depend heavily on their land to produce their annual supply of basic food: corn and beans. When times are hard, they sell their green beans and squash to resellers in the Oaxaca market. Animals serve as added economic insurance: their ducks, geese, turkeys, chickens, and pigs can be eaten, given to friends to fulfill personal obligations, or sold in a pinch.

Guillermina's family is central to all her efforts. Although she can't provide each of her children with living space and food, every one of them comes daily to help. When the land needs to be worked, her five sons head out to the fields early with her husband, making sure to return by midday so they still have energy left to work in clay. If there are no orders for ceramics, the children pick up whatever jobs they can find—in construction, in agriculture—"so that all the weight isn't on us." This is simply what being a family means.

Despite the continuing economic struggles, working with clay offers Guillermina a deeply emotional experience. "I think the more love one puts into the clay, the more beautiful it comes out. If you get angry, it doesn't come out well. The piece comes out crooked, it comes out badly." It is the intensity with which she feels both joy and sadness as she works that affects her most deeply: "The happiness comes from that moment you pour your heart into what you are creating. The sadness comes from then having to part with what you have just put so much love into." She looks wistful for a moment, then smiles: "To think, from that sadness and that joy, one earns a living!"

opposite:
Tree of Life
Guillermina Aguilar

Irene Aguilar

Doña Isaura's grave

Peace reigns in the municipal cemetery of Ocotlán, only a short block from the bustling town center. A handful of visitors kneel in prayer near their loved ones, or tend to their graves, replacing withered flowers with fresh bouquets. Irene Aguilar stands before the accomplishment that she is proudest of: the monument she has created to sit atop her mother's grave. Sheltered beneath a stately white dome on slim white pillars etched in gold, a ceramic Virgin appears both serene and spirited with golden crown, deep pink gown, flowing green robe, and arms laden with vibrantly colored flowers. Two angels perch on the roof of the dome, guarding the sanctaury below. A dramatic white and gold cross sits on the crest of the memorial.

After arranging large clusters of tall, velvety purple flowers on either side of this shrine to Isaura Alcántara, Irene carefully checks the inscription that has recently been engraved on the stone tablet blanketing the grave. She has composed it, with the help of her eldest son, Manuel:

> *Thank you for the creative spirit immortalized by your hands. A God-given marvel was your talent, although in life you were not given the honors you deserved because your name was unknown. Today your work is recognized internationally for sculpting our customs and traditions in clay. Through your own inventiveness and my hands, your greatness is preserved. You let your works be carried throughout the world in homage to you.*

Irene lets out a deep sigh of satisfaction. With this tombstone, she has finally been able to convey, and cancel, some of the debt she so intensely feels that she owes her mother for her magnificent gift of clay.

Irene has been unusually subdued during her visit to her mother's grave. As she slowly walks the five or so blocks back to her home at the entrance into town, her spirits lift. By the time she arrives at her front door, her usual exuberance and playfulness have returned. To the left of her outer wooden door, with its graceful iron knocker in the shape of a hand, a bench stands partly occupied by Irene's own creations. Stately fruit vendors have staked out space to hawk their wares. With papayas and watermelons on their heads, pineapples, grapes, and bananas packed on their shoulders, and slices of fruits dripping in their hands, the market women make a brilliant display in their skirts of pink, purple, blue, and red. They surround the artful sign, poised above the center of the bench, that reads: "Folk Art in Clay — Irene Aguilar and Children."

By the time she crosses her threshold, it would be hard for anyone to keep up with her. She has things to do! There is the rich black *mole* to be made in huge batches for her nephew's wedding. There are the final arrangements for this evening's performance of her daughter Nancy's dance troupe; traditional Oaxacan dances are one of Irene's great passions. Her spiritedness seems physically captured in the interior of the house. The expansive inner space bursts with color and animation. To the right of the threshold stretches a massive backcloth painted with a magnificent image of Christ on the Cross encircled by ascending angels. The wonderfully soft flesh tones of the angels, highlighted against the deep-blue background, intensify the dramatic scene. The set is the work of Irene's husband who, often with the help of their sons, constructs and paints elaborate scenery for religious festivals in the community.

To the left of the entrance is what Irene calls her "exhibition room." And while its shelves and center table hold many of her imaginative designs, a sultry ceramic platinum blonde dominates the room. With her slinky black skirt and skimpy gold top, she exudes lewdness. The cigarette dangling from her lipstick-smeared mouth adds to the effect. But this *dama de la noche* —woman of the night—

**Irene Aguilar
with her fruit vendors**

surprisingly also reflects her maker's playful humor. Irene keeps the figure, one of the first *damas* she ever did, because it prompted her first invitation to exhibit in the United States, more than a decade ago. Immediately behind this display area is a smaller room, the workshop where she does all her work in clay. She enters it now.

Calling for her younger son, Juan Carlos, twenty-five, and her daughter, Nancy, twenty-four, to help her, she smooths the moist torso of a large market woman that she had finished shaping earlier this morning. Usually she leaves her pieces, after they are formed, in a corner of this room to dry. After three or four days, longer during rainy season, they go off to the kiln for firing. But with large figures like this one, almost four feet tall, the pieces have to be moved while moist and put directly in the unlit kiln for a few days to dry. To move them after drying would chance the risk of cracking. When her children come in, she explains the task. Orchestrating the move, she ushers her children, and the figure, out.

She has one last task here before she can attend to the *mole* and the dance troupe. Inspired by *las chinas oaxaqueñas*, the female dancers who perform Oaxacan folk dances, she has created a set of them in clay. With the figures already fired, and most of them painted, Irene now concentrates on putting the finishing touches on the last dancer. With her paintbrush, she dabs an intricate pattern of fine white dots on the bright yellow ruffled skirt, replicating the embroidery of the authentic costume. She next colors the ribbon in the dancer's hair a vivid red, taking care not to discolor the traditional dark *rebozo* slung casually over the girl's shoulder. Irene's last chore is the elaborate floral arrangement in the basket that the dancer has expertly poised on her head. Finally, after dabbing the last fleck of orange into the folds of a calla lily, she straightens up to survey her work. A smile spreads broadly across her face. "I like my work!" she announces with great gusto to the room. She pauses, then tries again. This time she shouts jubilantly into the air, "I love my work!"

Nine years younger than Guillermina, Irene states, with characteristic directness, "I am a more modern woman." She has clipped her traditional braids, wears makeup often and, in general, takes a much more relaxed approach to the dress code traditionally demanded of Oaxacan women. "There are those women, like my sister, who are so accustomed to their apron and their *rebozo* that they feel naked if they go out without them. It's a habit imposed on them, or they have imposed it on themselves." Irene also enjoys wearing traditional clothing, especially her shawl, and always takes it with her when she travels because it is "part of my home."

She also has a much more pragmatic approach to running her household. Given the pace of her life, she has easily adapted to embracing convenience over convention. Before, if the firewood was wet, she would have to wait to make a fire to cook. "Now one only lights a match on the stove and there it is!" Before, she used to make salsa in the *molcajete*, the traditional stone mortar used to grind food by hand. "Now you just boil the tomato and the chile and you put it in the blender and in a second you have the salsa. Of course," she adds, "it doesn't have the same flavor." But then she laughs. "No, but you eat it if you're hungry!"

Still, Irene's life has been molded by the traditional burdens placed on young girls, as much as her clay figures are formed by her own hands. "There were so many of us. And my mother had to care for all of us; the girls had to help her.

opposite:
Ladies of the Night
Irene Aguilar

**Las Chinas Oaxaqueñas:
Festival Dancers**
Irene Aguilar

That's why I didn't go to school for very long. I only went for less than a year—less than a year!" While her brothers had household tasks, mainly getting the clay and the firewood, the workload fell most heavily on Irene and her sisters. "In my house, you worked from the moment you could walk." To make the family's tortillas, she had to get up at 4:30 A.M. and take the *nixtamal*, the mixture of corn kernels and lime, that she'd boiled the night before, to the mill to be ground into tortilla dough, the *masa*. She then spent hours making kilo after kilo of tortillas for the family. "By ten in the morning, you had worked yourself to death, but the tortillas were done." After the tortillas, there was the work in clay, and then sweeping and throwing out the trash, and then cleaning up the messes from her father's donkeys and dogs. Each day would end, by 8 P.M. if she was lucky, only when she prepared the next morning's *nixtamal*. "It was a brutal routine."

She had loved school, but had to leave to take care of her younger brother. "How I hated that baby. I didn't know that it wasn't his fault. I was only eight or nine, and I would pinch him and take his diapers off roughly. I spent a lot of years with the idea that it was his fault they had taken me out of school."

Irene knows that today many people assume she has studied a great deal. Early on she set out to learn whatever she could from any source, whether from magazines that caught her attention, or from people she talked to. Talking with older people especially helped. "My wisdom comes from the fact that I liked to talk to older people. I tell my children that old folks don't talk just to be annoying. They only talk because they *know*. So I talked a lot with older people. Even today I like to talk with them, to see what experiences they had. And from there you go learning the experiences of life." The experiences of everyday life thus became the real source of her education.

Although Irene's first efforts in clay, at the age of eight, produced work that she now calls "deformed," her skill, under her mother's tutelage, developed substantially by her teen years. But Doña Isaura's illness, when Irene was sixteen, dramatically changed her life. Her older sisters, Guillermina and Josefina, were already married with children of their own. It fell to her to shoulder the burden of caring for her mother, her younger siblings, and to find a way to pay for the medicine to control her mother's pain. She began to produce and sell clay figures on her own, finding that the group scenes or *juegos* that her mother had made—weddings, baptisms, funerals—sold best. She took her mother's death hard the following year.

Irene's marriage, and the birth of her first child at the age of twenty-one in 1972, temporarily interrupted the development of her career. The extreme hardship of her youth made her determined to limit the number of children she had, but her husband at first insisted that she forgo her craft anyway. Irene explains how she was able to resume the work she had come to love: "He didn't change his mind, I changed it for him." When her husband was hospitalized suddenly, she went immediately to the government artisan agency, FONART, to arrange for her first loan, promising clay figures in return. She then went to the hospital and told her husband not to worry about his medical bills. "'But where are we going to get the money?' he asked. 'I already got it,' I told him. In amazement, he asked, 'how?' I answered him, 'with my hands.'"

During her husband's slow recuperation, he helped Irene and only returned to his own career as a carpenter when their three children were old enough to help her. He also paints signs and festival scenery, and creates the enormous papier-mâché puppets that adorn Oaxacan religious celebrations. Irene is the only sister

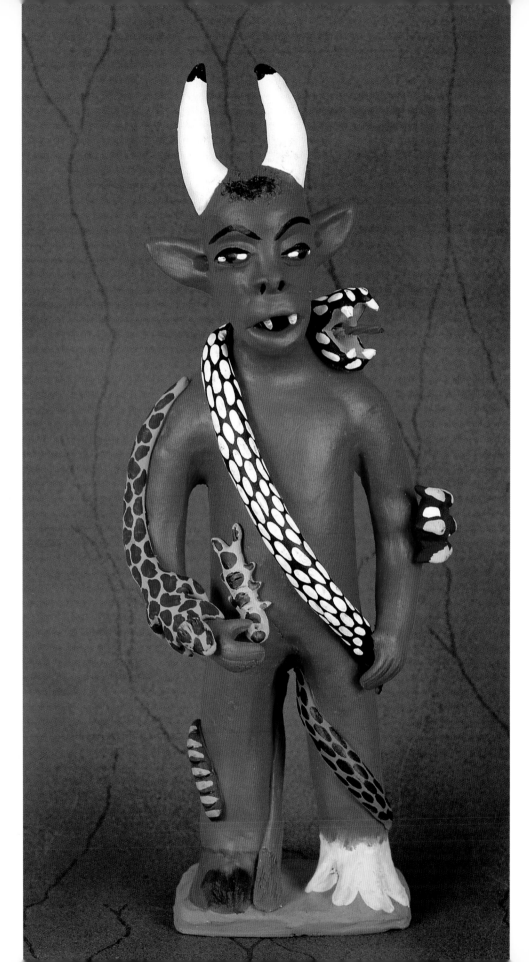

Devil
Irene Aguilar

44

whose husband provides an independent source of family income. But it is the degree of freedom he allows her to pursue her own career that is truly unusual in Oaxaca. "I found a man who understands me, who has guided me. But he respects my decisions. That is why I say that I found a good man."

Irene has sustained a long and illustrious career as a ceramist. In the early years, many of the Oaxacan shop owners and Mexican government organizations who were devotees of her mother's work helped her. By buying her work, arranging expositions and even giving financial assistance during tough times, they allowed her the opportunity to perfect her craft. During the 1980s, she began to win a host of Oaxacan and national competitions for her clay designs, including special recognition in 1981 from the National Museum of Popular Arts and Industries for her fifteen years of work as a folk artist. Since the first award ("I almost fainted!"), she has become more accustomed to the many prizes and awards that have since come her way. In 1986, she was invited to exhibit in the United States for the first time. The decade of the 1990s brought more honors. She won first place in 1997 and 1998 in the annual state ceramic competitions held in Oaxaca. She continues to accumulate awards for her clay figures from the Mexican government, private cultural foundations, and international corporations. And exhibitions of her work in the United States and Canada have increased.

Irene is very aware that she has traveled distances more vast than her trips outside of Oaxaca. "When I was young," she remembers, "we didn't have shoes and we walked around barefoot, without sweaters or even a shawl to keep us warm." She credits her mother's gift to her for the fullness of her life now. "Because of my mother's work, I have this place to live. Because of my mother's work, I have traveled; I have seen the world. Because of my mother's work, I have won prizes, I have had triumphs, I have gained knowledge." She adds in a hushed tone: "When my mother was dying, she'd say to me, 'When you marry and have a house, I am going to send you my blessings.' She really did. She has blessed me."

Concepción Aguilar

With a small, worn piece of felt cut from a man's sombrero, Concepción Aguilar smooths the clay wheels below the figure she has just formed. She is elated because this is the first time she has shaped this image in clay, inspired by a picture of the painter Frida Kahlo in a wheelchair. Doing a new piece gives her such a wonderful feeling of accomplishment, she explains, like when the man came years ago about Frida in the first place. He told Concepción who Frida was, that people liked her a lot in the United States, that there were Fridas on every kind of thing—on tee shirts, silverware, you name it. He asked her to make Fridas in clay, and brought a book with pictures of Frida and her paintings.

How that book opened her eyes! She could see how the real Frida was—her distinctive eyebrows, her love of traditional Indian clothes and jewelry. But the picture images had helped her even more in letting her imagination fly, to create the

Concepción Aguilar

Fridas as she fancied them, like the pieces she had finished painting yesterday. Concepción now glances at the shelf across the room, where her three Fridas stand. One is elegant in black *rebozo*, sapphire blue skirt, and chunky silver earrings. Another has a monkey and a parrot perched on her shoulders. The third, in bright red shawl and intricately patterned floral skirt, holds a dignified pose.

Concepción's elation contrasts sharply with her meager surroundings. As she rises out of her chair to put the fresh clay Frida on the shelf to dry, the faded print curtain on her right, which serves as the door to her home, flutters with her movement. In contrast to her sisters, she does not own her home. This is the seventh house she has rented as a married woman; she and her three daughters all dislike the frequent moves. And even though they always set the rough, handmade sign with her name in front, the changing locations confuse visitors and potential buyers. Still, the family does like this new home; they are right next door to Josefina. Their last home was off the main road, and it came with the added obligation to tend the owner's chickens and ducks. The animals were a nuisance, a filthy nuisance.

The room that Concepción is in serves as the living, sleeping, eating, and working space for her entire family. The house includes a passageway in which they cook, and part of a patio beyond that. It is a cramped space, with a double bed in the far left corner, a table with TV opposite the curtained entrance, and a few small tables arranged along the walls. Her husband uses one of these when he helps her paint her figures. Another holds finished items for sale. Concepción herself works at the table to the left of the entrance; when she is not working, the table is cleared for family meals.

The room is brightened by the vivid colors of Concepción's pieces and the bright red plastic chair she sits in to work. Above the television, a picture of her eldest daughter, Guadalupe Isaura, hangs proudly on the wall. Below it, a small, sparse altar has been arranged between the TV and the Fridas, flowergirls, and Virgins awaiting buyers. A candle glows next to a picture of the eight-month-old grandson, her first grandchild, who died recently. Her grandparents had taught her the importance of perpetual candle-light in an altar and she continues this tradition—so that God does not forget her family. She adds flowers when she can.

Three Fridas
Concepción Aguilar

Concepción sits down again at her work table; her delight over her new accomplishment aside, she is very tired. It is rare that she is home without her family, and she gives herself a few moments of quiet to ease her exhaustion from the work of the night before. She'd gotten home at two in the morning, tired not just from the late hour but from the tension she always feels when firing her pieces. With no kiln of her own, she has to borrow Irene's when it is not in use. Usually in Oaxacan potting families, like her sisters', husbands and sons are responsible for the firing process. But with no sons, and a husband who is frequently away, Concepción often has to take care of this herself.

The kiln is, for her, the hardest part of working with clay. In an instant, if the fire builds too quickly or becomes too hot, the figures can shatter. It had taken her half a year in the beginning to learn how to fire, and even then, she'd still some-times lose pieces. It is not only a big financial loss when figures break—the clay, the firewood, her time and labor, but an emotional disappointment too—especially if the pieces are beautiful. Now she has enough experience to ensure that her work comes out fine most of the time. But she still hasn't found the exact firing point for really big pieces, like the ones she fired last night. And even with smaller figures, the need

The Parrot Vendor
Concepción Aguilar

to constantly watch the fire always drains her. As she stirs to begin to work again, she reminds herself out loud that last night's firing was a success. She had checked again this morning, as the pieces still cooled in the kiln. She smiles, lets out a deep sigh, and reaches for her book on tropical rain forest animals.

Intently poring over the pictures, Concepción searches the pages for inspiration. She of course enjoys using the traditional themes of her mother and sisters, particularly the many Virgins of their faith. But there is something about the challenge of creating something novel that simply moves her. The few picture books she has, in a neat pile on the dirt floor near her feet, help a lot. Even before she started doing the clay Fridas, she had seen pictures of Diego Rivera's peasant women laden with calla lilies and had loved transforming that image into clay. This newer book on animals helped too. She learned about all sorts of creatures she had never seen. The awareness allowed her to create new compositions, like her distinctive Noah's ark, whose paint was still drying in front of the TV. The turquoise boat is filled with creatures real and imagined: a snake in primary colors slithers on top of a log on the ark's rim; an inquisitive skunk peers from one of its hollows, a lavender and pink elephant peeks from another. Bunches of ripe strawberries, bananas, and apples hang beside Noah, who strikes a relaxed pose on the boat's side. Striding atop the ark is an armadillo, bedecked in a fancy shell whose elaborate design is meticulously painted in green, red, pink, and yellow.

Concepción continues to turn pages, her eyes focusing with intense concentration on the passing images. She looks for the glimmer of a new theme that her hands can shape in clay, but one that she can paint in solid tones. While she loves the new elaborate style of painting she had recently developed for her arks, and her flowergirls, with their intricately patterned animals and flowers, it exhausted her to spend the whole day it took to paint a piece in that style. For several minutes, the rustling of pages is the only sound in the room. Suddenly that soft crackling stops too. "A parrot vendor!" she exclaims, spellbound by a vividly colored picture of parrots. She had never done that before. As she thinks more about this idea, her face becomes flushed with excitement. But how would a market woman manage to contain the birds? With the challenge of figuring out how to cage them, a smile of contentment plants itself on her face. She is lost, delightedly, in the possibilities.

Concepción Aguilar's face has a quiet grace—with the large eyes and high angular cheekbones reminiscent of 1940s movie stars. Neither her soft beauty nor her gracious manner reflect the difficult life she has led. At forty-two, she is the youngest Aguilar sister, and the one for whom life's struggles have been the most severe and unrelenting. "You see," she says matter-of-factly, "my life has hit me very hard."

She was ten when her mother died. Because her older sisters either were already married or soon left to marry, it fell to her to care for her father and two younger brothers: "I didn't have a childhood like some other kids, who have a mother, a father, who play, who laugh, who enjoy life, no." The difficulty of cooking, cleaning, and mothering the young boys was intensified by her father's heavy drinking.

Woman with Calla Lilies
Concepción Aguilar

These were years of sadness and suffering, and even though she would forage with her brothers for firewood to sell, they were years of hunger as well. "Tortillas with salt were all we ate. Sometimes tortillas with salsa and beans. When we had money, we bought beans and when we didn't, we didn't." It was her love for her brothers, and her deep sense of family duty, that kept her going: "Because those two little ones were there, I just had to fight to survive."

Even before her mother died, her household responsibilities made it unlikely that she could be spared to attend school. Once she had to care for the boys, schooling became impossible for her, even as she made sure that they attended primary school to become literate. When her father died in 1976, almost nine years after her mother, Oaxacan custom dictated that her brothers inherit the house and land that had been their father's inheritance before them. Concepción, by then nineteen, left to marry and begin her own family.

In those first years on her own, she did not have much interest in starting to work in clay. But like most *oaxaqueños*, she had to hustle to get by. She washed

other people's clothes; she worked for tailors in town, ironing the new pants they made; she embroidered for neighbors; she worked in a local restaurant, making food and waiting on tables. Even with all this scrambling, the few *pesos* she earned did not produce enough income. Economic necessity and "the urge" to return to her roots in clay soon propelled her to try her mother's craft when her first daughter, Lupe, was born in 1978.

In contrast to her sisters, Concepción learned to work in clay on her own. She did have memories of how her mother worked, since, as a child, she had often helped her. She had also learned a great deal over the years by watching her sisters create their own ceramic figures. But even as she began to develop her unique ceramic skills, she and her husband were too poor to buy the simple materials—clay, firewood, paint—necessary to work her craft full-time. It didn't help that some folk art stores in Oaxaca bought only on consignment from artisans or that she, as the youngest sister, never had the benefit of her mother's contacts in Oaxaca and elsewhere. She spent another decade continuing her other jobs, sporadically producing clay figures, sometimes even working for Guillermina and Irene when she needed cash.

Only in 1988, when she was thirty-one, was she able to devote herself full-time to working in clay. She began with the traditional motifs of her family, market women and Virgins, and the remarkable delicacy and grace of her figures quickly gained her recognition—and sales. Her Virgins especially reflect her exquisite talent: Concepción infuses them with such serenity and faith that they simply radiate spirituality. She very soon began to experiment with different themes, perhaps because the absence of tutelage by her mother left her free to innovate. "I have already come up with almost forty-five new items from my imagination," she beams. Two years after the decision to work in clay full-time, she received her first award from the National Museum of Popular Arts and Industries in Mexico City. Invitations to exhibit in the United States and Canada came shortly after.

With the decision to devote herself to ceramic work, Concepción has entered a new phase in her life, finding some degree of personal satisfaction and economic stability for the first time. "The work is beautiful," she exclaims, adding that another pleasurable advantage of working in clay, in contrast to her previous work, is that "here one is the boss and the worker at the same time." Using the haunting measure of her childhood, her life today brings a kind of comfort never

Crying Angel
Concepción Aguilar

opposite:
Shepherd
Concepción Aguilar

attained before: "This has worked out for us because, while we don't live great, we have enough to eat, and that is most important."

Hardships continue, with no home, land, or even kiln of her own. Things are particularly tough during those months of the year when few tourists come to buy, Oaxacan galleries cut back on their orders because of low sales, and stores from elsewhere don't buy either. During these times, she sometimes can't even afford to buy paint.

But despite the continuing vulnerabilities that have marked her whole life, Concepción builds joyfulness into her days much as she creates exuberance and gaiety in her folk art from mere water and the earth. In her three daughters, she has always found delight, as well as an important source of help with all her chores ("That's what daughters are for"). In the rich ceremonial life of Ocotlán, she always finds a break from work and woes. She participates with gusto in community festivals and celebrations, to revel in seeing her daughters dancing and having the fun she never was allowed as a young girl, as much as for her own enjoyment.

In her religious commitment, she finds deep comfort: "When I see that I have a big, big problem, I go to church and ask for help. It's as if I get out of those problems faster than I can imagine. It's like they say, no? That faith can move mountains."

In her extended family, she also finds assistance and support. She has been sustained at important times in her life by the generosity of her sisters. Although there are, at times, the natural tensions stemming from the sisters' competitive location in the same economic niche, and their physical location next door to one another, family ties continue to bind them together. Concepción and her girls have lived with Irene for short periods during difficult times. Josefina and her husband José were recently the godparents of daughter Estela's wedding, and before that they sponsored the youngest daughter Gabriela's fifteenth birthday celebration. Guillermina's daughters are godmothers of important events in their three cousins' lives.

Then there is the clay itself. In her work she finds both beauty on a daily basis and hope for the future. Her ceramic figures hold out the promise of fulfilling her deepest yearning. "My greatest wish is that we could buy a little piece of land. Land is the most important thing because then you can build a house—out of sheet-metal or whatever." Perhaps, she reasons, when she has worked with clay as long as her sisters, she too will be able to buy some land. Then she would not have to move anymore, and her daughters would have some security after her death. This is the legacy, beyond that of clay, that she would like to pass on to her daughters. It is the clay that allows her to dream.

opposite:
Noah's Ark
Concepción Aguilar

Santa María Atzompa

For Angélica Vásquez and Dolores Porras, their artisanal inheritance comes as much from a village as from family. Each had potters as parents, but both women were also able to use the resources of an entire community to develop their skills. In contrast to Ocotlán, where only the Aguilar sisters and a few other women make their living as ceramists, Santa María Atzompa is a major pottery-producing center in the state of Oaxaca, where virtually everyone's hands are in clay.

That pottery is Atzompa's business is seen just about everywhere in the village. Women burdened with dozens of earthenware pots walk, heads down, determined to reach their destination quickly, children scurrying after them, trying to keep up. Matrons stand patiently in the plaza, large *ollas* on the ground in front of them, waiting for buyers. Armloads or headloads of pottery are glimpsed fleetingly down every path or bend in the road. Large circular adobe kilns peep from behind cactus fences, commanding presences in the midst of courtyards strewn with debris.

Atzompa has been producing pottery since the time of the great Zapotec civilization that dominated the valley centuries earlier; many of the clay vessels that the village produces today have pre-Columbian roots. Pottery has survived across the centuries as the economic mainstay of the community no doubt because of the local lack of rich, arable land. What land individual *atzompeños* may own is rarely irrigated, and although the village itself holds substantial communal land, having to depend on rain for crops makes too shaky a basis for real sustenance.

Even with the availability of cheap plastic dishes, Atzompa has been able to maintain its position as the major supplier of domestic pottery for the region. The demand for its ware continues because the inexpensive clay pots and dishes that it makes are still used daily by villagers throughout the valley of Oaxaca and even beyond. *Atzompeños* themselves use the earthenware only from their own village. The continuing importance of the historic market system of the valley—with different weekly *mercados* in villages spread widely through the area—has probably encouraged the use of traditional forms of pottery and provided an outlet for their sale. The very nearness of Oaxaca de Juárez, the state capital, only a few miles away, provides an especially important opportunity to sell at its huge Saturday market.

The closeness of the city of Oaxaca makes a visit to Atzompa jarring, for the village has the feel of a rural community far removed from urban ways. It is not just the poverty, though the unpaved streets patterned with the gullies of last year's rain serve as a reminder of scarce resources. Pottery does not make a village rich. Although villagers do not speak Indian dialects, tradition is as much in the air as potters' dust. The rich customs of the community have been maintained through the common ties of religion, fiestas, and clay.

If the past is present everywhere in Atzompa, so too are the inklings of change. Young people now leave on the bus for schooling outside. Store signs in faded pastels announce videos for rent alongside tortillas for sale. The images of women, in particular, visually suggest the mosaic of different eras that simultaneously exist on Atzompa's streets. The older generation of women wear long cotton skirts, their hair in braids, and always, if outside their homes, the cloth symbol of matronly respectability, their apron, or *mandil*. Most women, even younger ones who have discarded their mothers' ankle-length skirts, sport the ubiquitous dark cotton or silk *rebozo* inventively draped to serve many needs: shawl-like for carrying babies or casseroles, twisted turban-like on the top of the head to shield from the glaring sun. A few women even manage to navigate the stones and rubble in heels, having swapped shawls for sweaters and their *mandil* for mascara.

The ceramic work of both Angélica Vásquez and Dolores Porras is deeply rooted in the distinctive pottery styles for which Atzompa is famous. The village, interestingly, is not identified with just one type of pottery. It produces, for example, unglazed earthenware pottery for everyday use in a variety of shapes: the *comal*, the clay griddle for tortillas, the all-purpose *apaxtle*, and the *cazuela* or casserole. It is especially famous for its *loza verde* or green-glaze ware, whose gleaming surface comes from the green metallic glaze first introduced by the Spanish. Although it looks only decorative, *loza verde* is, in fact, very strong, flame resistant, and waterproof. It is made in a wide range of shapes, the most distinctive being the special Atzompa *jarro* (jug) with its elongated neck and high handle, prized for making Mexican hot chocolate. The village is known for a number of ornamental items not related to cooking such as *macetas* or *jardineras* (flowerpots), and *floreros* (vases), which often serve religious purposes on private altars or in church.

Dolores Porras's storeroom

The village also has achieved renown for its *juguetes* or toys: miniatures of its pottery, tiny animals, and whistles, favored not only by children in the region, but by adults as well. Each of these types of pottery has helped to form the artistic style of Dolores's and Angélica's work in clay.

One cannot mention the pottery of Santa María Atzompa without also mentioning Teodora Blanco Núñez, the pioneering woman who fundamentally altered the kind of ceramic work *atzompeños* did. Of the same generation as Isaura Alcántara, she too died young, at the age of fifty-two, in 1980. But in contrast to Doña Isaura, Teodora's innovation and imagination made her the most famous potter that the village had ever produced. The legacy of her clay forms is a significant

**Peasant Woman
with Machete**
Angélica Vásquez

part of the community heritage that today shapes the creative output of Angélica Vásquez and Dolores Porras, who actually served as Teodora's assistant for many years.

Teodora Blanco was only a young teenager when she inventively created a totally new kind of *juguete*: animals playing musical instruments. These *músicos* proved so popular that everyone began making them. Drawing upon Atzompa's rich repository of animal myths, Teodora experimented with fantastic forms of jugs and pitchers, putting animal heads, tails, or wings on them. She became most famous for her large unglazed *muñecas*, or dolls, laden with elaborate clay "embroidery." This style of embellishing her figures with clay designs modeled in high relief had pre-Hispanic roots; Teodora revived the technique and applied it for the first time to the female figure.

Her inventiveness has had an immense influence on pottery in Atzompa. Her success initially shined the light of publicity on her village's ceramics. She was one of Nelson Rockefeller's favorite Mexican folk artists, and right on his heels soon followed the more general tourist public. In more subtle ways, her work continues to have an impact. Much like Doña Isaura, Teodora Blanco signaled the possibility—and legitimacy—of innovation. Her work provided an example of the creativity with which one could break away from traditional ideas about pottery, while using tradition to imagine new forms.

Like Teodora Blanco and other women in Atzompa from potter families, Angélica Vásquez learned to work in clay at her parents' side. From an early age, it was, literally, all around her. Her mother, Delfina Cruz Díaz, and her father, Ernesto Vásquez Reyes, are still active potters who have spent their entire lives working together making mainly *corriente*, everyday ware. They taught Angélica the techniques she needed to make simple shapes so that by the age of ten, she already had the skill to begin to create in her own style. Dolores Porras also benefited from a family with a tradition of working in *loza verde*, where she learned much about clay, firings, and glaze. But she takes fierce pride in being essentially self-taught. Abandoned by her mother when she was seven, Dolores grew up watching her father, stepmother, and maternal grandmother work but was not tutored by any one of them. Both Angélica and Dolores acknowledge the advantages of growing up with families whose lives revolved around the daily rituals of clay. But equally important are the ways in which their talents have been molded by location and place.

Dolores Porras's work draws upon all the styles for which Atzompa is famous. She makes glistening, colorful flowerpots and planters. Her years with Teodora Blanco gave her great skill in populating natural unglazed pots with slithery animals and creeping plants. In the tradition of innovation that Teodora Blanco symbolizes, Dolores has created new forms of pottery to add to Atzompa's standard repertory. As her work absorbs the legacy of Atzompa's pottery styles, she adapts them ingeniously to produce her own personal style.

Angélica Vásquez too has benefited from the abundant heritage of her village. Her extraordinary interest and skill in molding minute clay forms probably is rooted in Atzompa's *juguete* tradition of miniaturization. Her creative imagination has roots in Atzompa's myths and legends; like Teodora Blanco, she is inspired by visions of animal spirits that she captures in clay. But she has built upon the tradition of innovation to produce complex cultural compositions that, in their sophistication, surpass what has been made before. For Angélica, as for Dolores, the double inheritance of family and community has resulted in a uniquely personal and powerful *arte popular*.

Apaxtle **with Fish**
Dolores Porras

Dolores Porras

Dolores Porras, Atzompa's warmhearted pioneer of multicolored glazed pottery, is on her knees. With shoulders hunched and body tilted forward, she buries her hands in a mass of charcoal-gray clay. She massages the clay much the way she used to knead tortilla dough in her younger days or on special occasions now still kneads mounds of fragrant ground cacao beans, crushed almonds, sugar, and cinnamon to make Oaxacan chocolate. She folds, presses, and stretches the mass of clay again and again until, finally satisfied that it is pliable enough, she stops, falling back on her haunches to rest.

The simple tools that Dolores uses to make her ceramic designs surround her. An *apaxtle* with water rests at her knee. The small piece of wool, cut from a man's hat, that she uses to level and refine the surface of the clay slumps into the basin's side. A few broken pieces of gourd lie nearby: the smaller fragments will smooth the clay as she works, the larger, rounded pieces will help her plane the curved interior of larger pots as she builds up their sides. A long, spiny, cactuslike thorn lies in the dirt at her feet, ready to help her etch her ceramics with fine lines and details.

Directly in front of Dolores sit the two implements that have been characteristic of pottery-making in Atzompa for centuries: the *molde* and the *volteador*. The *molde* is a thick flat disk made of baked rough clay, on which the fresh clay is shaped; the *volteador* is the base, typically spherical and also made of baked clay, upon which the *molde* is balanced and rotated. While some women in the village specialize in the making of *moldes* because it is "an art," Dolores prefers to make her own. She also prefers her own version of the *volteador*—a rounded plate she flips over to use as the support for her *molde*. Together these implements allow Dolores to approximate a rudimentary version of a rotating wheel. The Spaniards introduced the potter's wheel into Mexico after the Conquest, but she, like generations of *atzompeñas* before her, continues to resist its use. Even now, the several potter's wheels in Atzompa, manual or electric, are used by men. Dolores views the foot motion required by the wheel as dangerous for women, citing a pregnant *atzompeña*, foolish enough to try the wheel, who recently miscarried for the third time.

With half a century's experience in molding clay, Dolores begins to work swiftly. Taking up long, fat ropes of clay she has previously shaped—*longas*, she calls them—her hands rapidly alternate between spinning the *molde* and build-

Pot with Angels
Dolores Porras

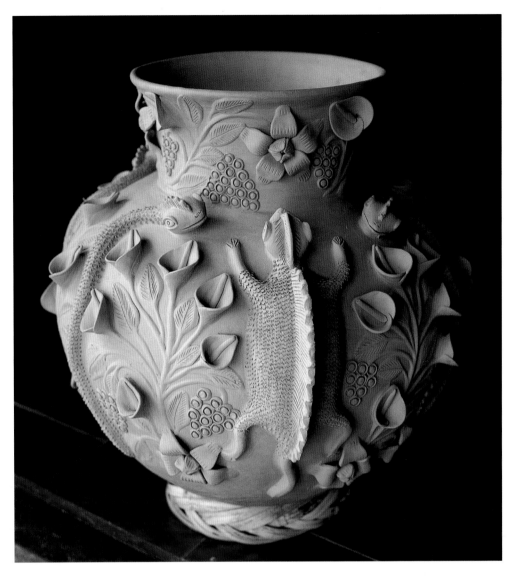

**Pot Embellished
with Flora and Fauna**
Dolores Porras

ing up the sides of the pot with the *longas*. If she is lucky enough to work the whole day with minimal interruptions—hard to achieve in a household with continual commotion—she will be able to complete six unadorned pots by dusk. But then she will spend two more days decorating them. For this order, from an old client, Dolores will wrap small protruding faces, molded in relief, around the curve of each pot. Although she calls this composition simply "pot with angels," the angels have a wild look, with piercing eyes and hair streaming out to the sides. The visual effect is almost Munch-like, as if her angels have been frozen in fright. The overall impression of the design, forged in the rough, stony medium of baked clay, is an intricate fusion of sophistication and naiveté, a blend characteristic of much of her work.

Dolores's ceramics are only occasionally figural; she is predominantly a potter, producing vessels, vases, platters, and plates that span the dual functions of practical home use and decoration. What is truly unusual is the breadth of different

pottery styles she is capable of producing. Now, as she continues to work intently, smoothing and refining the curved surface of the pot whirling in front of her, she is surrounded by some of the striking variety of clay pieces she creates. In front of her, awaiting packing, is an enormous unglazed clay pot, done in the *bordado* style popularized by Teodora Blanco. Dolores's clay "embroidery" expresses her own distinct style: Lizards and snakes weave silently among the lilies and grapes of a fantasy landscape. Lined up behind her, along the bedroom's outer wall, sit several examples of another of her signature pieces, decorated with raised stripes of yellow, brown, green, and blue undulating across the curved exterior of the pots. A few feet beyond, some large platters are propped against the wall, their pale, glazed surfaces populated with stylized fish in orange, blue, yellow, and green.

Dolores Porras

Despite the protection of the covered patio on which she works, streaks of dazzling sunlight begin to filter across Dolores's face—a full, round, expressive face, almost moon-shaped, framed by long salt-and-pepper braids which today are intertwined with hot pink ribbons and coiled on top of her head. Her ample frame is wrapped in a white apron brightened with delicate hand embroidery, the choice of dress reflecting the traditional pull of her generation: "If I walked around without an apron, people would look at me funny." Even though she will spend the entire day at home working with clay, she wears gold and pearl earrings cast in an old Oaxacan design, to complete the proper attire of a respectable matron in the community.

She looks up with a quick smile as her youngest child, Leticia, twenty-one, who Dolores had at forty-one, walks across the courtyard to join her. Of the eleven children she has given birth to, Leti is the only unmarried daughter among the nine still living. Leticia, who strongly resembles her mother, pulls a small chair under her body to sit, preferring it to the hard, cold floor where her mother, and countless generations of Oaxacan women potters before her, traditionally sit to mold clay. As Leticia plunges her fingers into the heap of moist clay, the two women begin to chat comfortably. Dolores's ringing tones and easy laughter rapidly fill the patio with a mood of relaxation and good cheer.

In front of them, the large courtyard sprawls messily toward the fenced entrance to the property alongside one of Atzompa's rutted dirt streets. Between Dolores and her daughter at one end, and the gate at the other, are piles of pottery of every description. Several unadorned pots await further decoration; stacks of finished planters stand ready to be shipped to a hotel on Oaxaca's west coast. Whitewashed vases, already fired once, wait for paint and glaze so they can be fired a second, final time. Dogs weave in and out of the pieces of pottery; a young pup tries unsuccessfully to interest his brother in a game. Near the front gate, a small

opposite:

Roped Pot
Dolores Porras

Vase with Fish
Dolores Porras

mountain of firewood partially blocks the way. Garbage is piled nearby. Broken fragments of pottery lie everywhere.

Other members of Dolores's household stand amidst the clutter, intently concentrating on their own tasks. Alfredo, her husband of forty-five years, focuses on packing pottery into two huge willow baskets for safe shipping. He was born and raised in this very courtyard, which he inherited after his father died. He and Dolores have finally been able to substitute a house of cinder block and cement for the cardboard hut thatched with sugarcane leaves that they'd lived in for years. Alfredo is especially proud of the newest addition: a workroom to provide cool refuge from the glaring sun, built where their burros used to be tethered. The burros had provided an important form of insurance: In bad times, Alfredo would load them all up at the clay mines, drop the clay they needed for themselves at home and go off to sell the rest. But the animals' deaths had freed up the space for this new room, even if Dolores was still upset about how they died: One strangled on his own rope and soon after all the others succumbed when their stomachs swelled.

Alfredo occasionally looks up from his own task to check the progress of his two married sons at the open-air kiln, only a few feet in front of the patio where Dolores is working. Norberto, twenty-eight, had been slowly calming the fire, but now both he and Bertín, twenty-seven, have become engrossed in taking the blistering pottery out with hooks. Timing is important, because glazed pieces must be removed quickly after their "second cooking" or else they will stick together, unlike unglazed pottery which can stay hours in the kiln cooling.

The sons, like their father, are engaged in the "men's work" in pottery making: getting and preparing the clay, handling the firewood, preparing with paint or glaze the pieces for firing, taking charge of the kiln, packing up the ceramics. As Alfredo puts it, "The woman understands the kitchen. We men, the firewood, the clay, all the preparation." While only Dolores, her daughters, and daughters-in-law actually work the fresh clay to form their creations, the men of the family play an important role in the ceramic process. This was one reason why it did not please Alfredo one bit that their first seven offspring were girls. Thank goodness they managed finally to have three sons!

As the day progresses, Dolores's household settles into a rhythm of easy-going bustle. Two of her five married daughters—all have separate households in Atzompa, with their own kilns—stop by to chat. Grandchildren play in the courtyard, inventing their own games. Occasionally a taxi pulls up to the gate, with tourists from Mexico City or the United States who have come to buy. Dolores rushes to attend to them. Throughout the busy activity, there is an ambience of good humor, relaxed chatter, and much laughter. Life has not always been so tranquil for Dolores Porras.

"When I remember the life I went through, and I remember what we suffered, everything, it makes me very sad." Dolores still finds it hard to talk about the first decades of her life. Her mother simply left one day, leaving Dolores, at seven, with a baby half-brother to care for. Although she lived with her father and his legal wife, her mother's older sister, she was never treated as a member of their family. She cooked and cleaned for them, was sent on odd jobs to earn her keep, but often had to depend upon the kindness of neighbors for food. Her mother soon returned to the village, but never attempted to contact her. Even now, a grandmother in her sixties, Dolores's eyes fill with tears at the memory of this indelible loss, the mother whose path she still crosses in Atzompa, but who has never acknowledged her.

Her marriage at seventeen to Alfredo, whom she had known since childhood, did not provide the escape from poverty she had hoped for. Although she worked hard producing the green-glazed cookware she had learned to make as a child, the pennies earned did not provide enough even for food. She began to have her children—all delivered "by my own strength and pure will," she says proudly—but their dire situation forced her to return to her clay within hours of each time she gave birth. Their first two children died, Dolores and Alfredo now say, because of "ignorance and poverty." When these daughters became ill, the first at eight months, the second at three years, there was no money to even attempt to cure them.

Troubles eased somewhat when Alfredo, in the 1960s, got a job at a nearby sawmill. Yet even with Dolores also working, making *loza verde* at a brother's house

Urn with naked figure and flying hair, fired once, awaiting painting and second firing
Dolores Porras

in the morning and at an uncle's house in the afternoons, there wasn't enough for clothing or shoes for the children. Sometimes, by late afternoon, there would still be a frantic search for money for food.

But pottery held the promise of salvation. By the 1970s, both Dolores and Alfredo were working for Teodora Blanco. Dolores made the bodies of the *muñecas*, or large clay dolls, for Teodora to decorate; Alfredo helped with sweeping or firing the kiln. With their combined pay less than fifty cents a day, Dolores continued to mold her own ware, and on weekends the couple would wind their way along the Río Atoyac to the market area in Oaxaca to sell. By the late seventies, Dolores fortuitously began to experiment with other forms of pottery, in addition to Atzompa's traditional green crockery. Perhaps inspired by her experience with Teodora Blanco, she created unglazed planters in the shape of turtles. With the move beyond *loza verde*, things began to change.

Dolores working in her courtyard

The turning point came after the painter Roberto Donís placed an order for planters, after seeing Dolores's turtle pots at the house of a friend. He asked if Alfredo and Dolores could come to Oaxaca to collect the money for the order, at the Rufino Tamayo Fine Arts Workshop, which he helped found. In Atzompa, potters always created either natural unglazed earthenware or the typical green-glazed ware. Seeing the painters at work was a revelation to Alfredo and Dolores, and they left the workshop excited by a new idea. "My husband said, 'And why can't we paint the clay?'" Dolores recalls. She remembers answering, "Well, we'll have to make the effort."

And they did make the effort, despite numerous hurdles along the way. The question of what type of paint to use was solved by an old client who sent samples from Monterrey. There were difficulties of trial and error; at first they used only two colors, red and white, but gradually they expanded to a multitude of hues. They soon discovered they had to fire their pieces twice, using a variety of washes, paints, and glaze to achieve the brilliant baked colors they sought. Dolores developed her own design ideas as they experimented with technique, acquiring particular fondness for images of mermaids, salamanders, iguanas, and native flowers. With help, they overcame the initial doubts of store owners, who were hesitant to try to sell a type of pottery so new. Eventually their persistence reaped rewards. The multicolored clay pottery they pioneered has become as synonymous with Atzompa as its traditional green-glazed ware.

Dolores's trendsetting work established her career. A first-place award in a state ceramic competition in 1984 became the first of several. Her ceramics began to be exhibited in Oaxaca, Mexico City, and other locations throughout Mexico.

Buyers soon came from the United States, Canada, Europe, and Japan, as well as from within Mexico. "They liked this work because it was new," she says modestly. With the attention, she finally dared to give up making and selling *loza verde*, for more than thirty years her bread-and-butter security. But she did continue to produce creative designs in natural, unglazed earthenware, which also found favor. In 1989, accompanied by Alfredo, Dolores took her first trip outside Mexico to Santa Fe, New Mexico, to demonstrate her skills. "We went alone, like adventurers," she remembers, still thrilled by the thought of their daring. Since then, she and Alfredo have become accustomed to travel to the United States, making several more trips to New Mexico, Texas, and Montana to exhibit her work.

Platter with Fish
Dolores Porras

Ironically, Dolores's success brought with it a new set of worries. In a pottery community like Atzompa, where nearly everyone faces an ongoing struggle for survival, the perception that Dolores has had her triumphs has created a backlash. The leveling norms of the village, with its "let's give others a chance" creed, resulted in Dolores's exclusion from participation in the artisan market recently organized in town to attract tourists. Worse yet, copies of her work pop up everywhere. As tourist traffic beelines to the centrally located handicrafts market or to the stores along the main street that now sell work similar to her own, fear of the poverty that has haunted Dolores throughout her life often returns.

But so do the resourcefulness and the energy that have propelled her life forward. Dolores prays hard for some security in her future, but she also believes "the Blessed Mother isn't just going to bring us things." Alfredo chimes in: "We also have to put our peas in the pot." Dolores nods her head in vigorous agreement with her husband, while reaching for some more clay. She smiles broadly, repeating with emphasis, "We have to work!"

Angélica Vásquez

It is Sunday and 103 degrees in the noontime sun, but this is no day of rest for Angélica Vásquez. Despite the stifling heat and the glaring sunlight, she moves quickly around the circular adobe kiln in her parents' courtyard, tucking shards of broken pottery in between the dozens of pots she and her parents have already artfully stacked in the kiln's depths. She radiates energy and competence as she races through the preparations for the firing to begin. Most of the chores are second nature to her: She grew up with clay, making small pots by the age of seven and experimenting with her own designs by ten. The childhood years spent watching her father preparing the clay and firing the kiln helped her garner skills beyond the molding process. Adult need honed her skills further: As a divorced mother of young children, she had no alternative but to run the kiln herself.

It has been decades since she lived with her parents—she married at fifteen—but she uses their kiln these days because she does not like the flame her own oven puts out. Until she can build another, she prefers the large, well-made kiln here in her childhood home. Arranging her parents' sturdy cooking ware around the inside perimeter of the kiln, she makes sure to leave a space for her own more delicate figures in the middle—a position close to the flame that also ensures a perfect clarity to the rich earthen tones of her unglazed pieces once they emerge from the heat.

Angélica's mother, Delfina, joins her at the kiln, revealing two different generations of Oaxacan women: The mother in her apron, her sun-weathered face protected by the *rebozo* folded in layers on her head; the daughter in print blouse and straw hat to ward off the searing sun. Both women ignore the perspiration streaming down their faces as they expertly complete the preparations for firing. Some eighty pots have already been tightly stacked—the better to hold in the heat—with the larger, simpler clay pots placed on the bottom and smaller or more decorative vessels layered successively until almost even with the top of the kiln.

Classy Lady
Angélica Vásquez

Angélica reaches for the last of her pieces still warming on the rim, the figure of an angel whose front is adorned with the tiny figures of a wedding scene, and nestles it into the one remaining space in the center, amongst the shards. As she clasps the angel in her hands, she carefully gauges the temperature of the dried clay. Warming her pieces in the sun before firing is an essential part of the process: If not

Angélica Vásquez

warmed sufficiently, the pieces can explode in the oven. Usually she will bathe her figures in the sun for at least five or six hours; in today's scorching heat, she expresses confidence that three hours are enough.

With the kiln full, she and her mother now move quickly around its perimeter, covering the top layer of pots with what appear to be numerous *comales*, the clay griddles used everywhere in Mexico for tortillas. In fact, these round clay pieces are covers made especially for the kiln, forming a shield that helps to retain the heat and repel potentially damaging intrusions, like rain. As the last *comal* is put in place, Angélica rapidly surveys the surface of the kiln, double-checking that the preparations are complete. Now the firing can begin.

As she mounds some firewood near her feet, Angélica swiftly cracks thin twigs over her knee. Her actions in overseeing the firing are unusual for a woman in Oaxaca, where men typically take charge of firewood and flame. But independence from traditional expectations is nothing new to her. She was, after all, the child who started her own business, making and selling clay toothpick holders and crocheted glass covers, in order to buy (by thirteen!) her own sewing machine ("I wanted to be a great person, a dress designer"). Spunk and determination have been her hallmarks: "What I have thought all my life, since I was a child, is that you only need a little interest and some gumption and you can get ahead." Unfortunately for her, gumption is not particularly valued as an attribute of women in Atzompa.

Country Girl
Angélica Vásquez

Angélica begins to fire with a slow flame, using what is referred to as "garbage" for fuel. Burned when an intense fire is not needed, the "garbage" is almost always plant matter, such as dried grasses—easier to find and cheaper than firewood. Today Angélica uses the large, bulbous roots of a native reed plant to provide the initial slow buildup of heat necessary during the first hour of firing. When her fingertips can no longer bear to touch the top of the kiln, she reaches for the firewood, steadily feeding the fire and intensifying the flame. While using the kiln in the heat of the day is uncomfortable, it is wind, not heat, that plays havoc with the firing process. Any breeze can shift the flame, making the firing uneven. Angélica remains vigilant, adeptly using a hook to move the wood, making sure the flame is not thrown by the air to one side, overfiring some

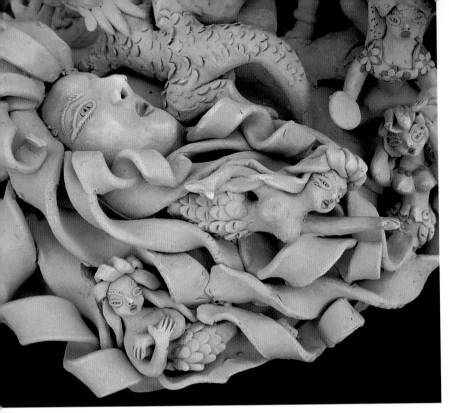

detail above, and opposite:
**Virgins, Mermaids, and
Market Women**
Angélica Vásquez

pieces while underfiring others. Three hours after she has begun, she lets the fire die out. She is as baked as her ware, but satisfied: "They are hard jobs but I do them with joy because I learned to do them well. I feel a little proud in that sense."

Angélica chats briefly with her parents, telling them she will be back after the kiln cools down to help unload, and turns briskly onto the dusty road toward home. It is a long, hard, uphill climb, but she strides energetically, as if the demanding work of the last few hours had not tired her in the least. A bare ninety pounds, her slight frame misleadingly suggests frailty and an almost adolescent youthfulness that conceals her forty-one years. In many ways, this difficult walk from her childhood home down below, and on the very edge of town, up to her new house near the top of the hill serves as a metaphor for much that she has experienced in her life.

While her childhood was not easy—"We grew up without a single toy and very little food, we were completely poor"—she remembers it as "a beautiful period for me." Loving, kind parents and a special relationship with her maternal grandmother, who regaled her with magical stories of Oaxacan lore, nourished her spirit. The physical freedom she and her siblings were allowed helped too: "We ran around like goats in the fields—free, free! There were big trees and we could find armadillos, possums, owls—all those animals lived there. That was our joy, instead of toys."

The really cruel years for her came after her marriage: "My life fell apart and I lost everything. I lost even my work with clay." Her husband, a mere sixteen, took her to live in his parents' compound, not far from her own parents. During their ten years together he would periodically disappear; one year after their fourth child was born, he abandoned her permanently. She later learned that he had run off with another woman to the United States. Left without money, with her baby seriously ill and hospitalized, she had to sell her belongings to pay for her son's care. Her in-laws would not help: "They said it was my fault their son had left. So they didn't speak to me at all, for more than a year." Left in the midst of this hostile camp, her own parents too poor to take her back, Angélica struggled to provide for her children. There were "many stones in my path," but she was determined to succeed—and to achieve some independence as a female, in spite of the obstacles.

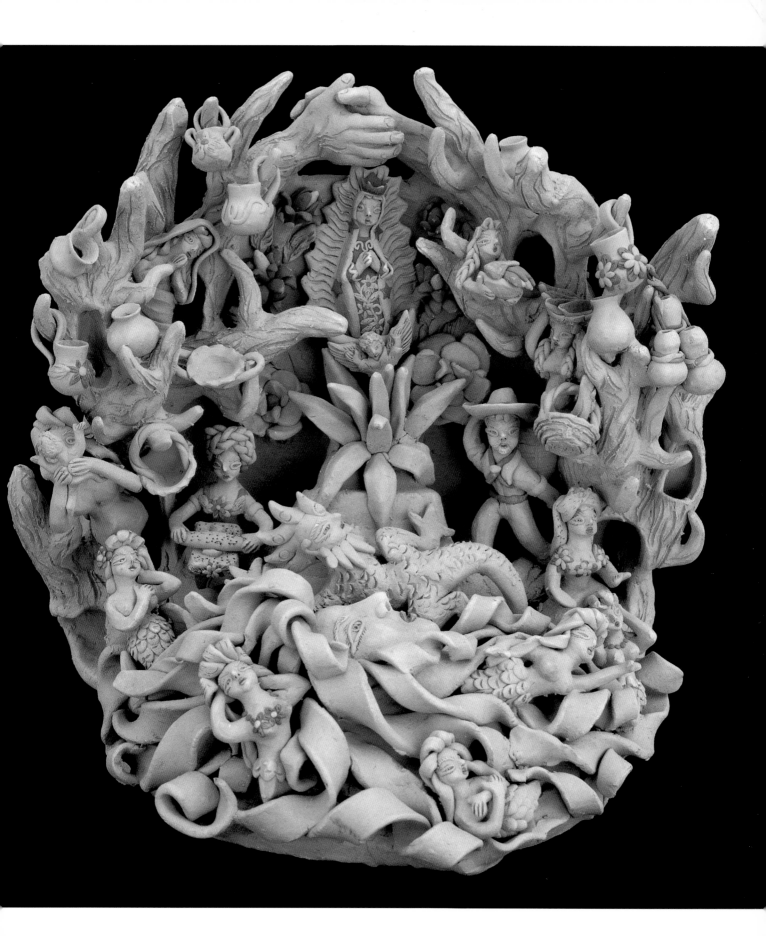

Now dodging the actual rocks in the rutted road and the thin, mangy dogs that straggle in and out of open gates, Angélica soon reaches her home, painted a vivid sky blue that blends with the expanse above, and opens the gate. After the arid dust of the trek up, she enters into an oasis of green, created, in her usual fashion, though grit and hard work. Six years ago this courtyard was barren land; now there is a profusion of budding trees, lush plants, and brilliant flowers. Purple trumpets fan across the blue wall on her right as she mounts the few stairs to the cool shade of the enclosed patio, where her two daughters and two sons are absorbed in Sunday chores. Assuring herself that they do not need her help, she turns into the entrance of the room off the patio that serves as her studio.

The large room is almost bare of furniture, with shelves in one corner displaying Angélica's clay creations—individual figures or sculpted compositions, not vessels—in varying stages of completion. Scattered around the room also are several tall earthenware planters, imaginatively shaped as women in traditional Oaxacan dress, made by her parents. Angélica has recently been tutoring them in new designs and techniques, hoping to encourage them to make more salable popular art, in addition to their cookware. "They have been working many years and they

Miniature Dancers
Angélica Vásquez

haven't seen the horizon that is behind the hill." She keeps the finished planters to help sell them; collectors and tourists frequently make their way here, while her parents are unknown.

Angélica now arranges herself directly on the floor, legs curled under her to one side, and reaches under the protective plastic sheet at her side for some fresh clay. Hardly glancing down, as if her hands had a mind of their own, she swiftly molds minuscule figures for one of her signature pieces: an angel whose arching wings enclose a Lilliputian nativity scene. When she is done, some twenty forms, some no bigger than a thumbnail, will encrust the angel's front. Technically demanding in both scale and content, her ceramic designs require an uncommon mastery of technique, which she has amply acquired. Over a decade ago, she already had won a national award for technical excellence in ceramics.

Although the raw clay she now works is a deep charcoal gray, when the piece is fired, it will emerge from the kiln a light, natural hue, in a range from cream to deep beige, depending on the figure's position in the kiln and the intensity of heat on its surface. Since she neither paints nor glazes her pieces, Angélica often uses a second color of clay, which, when fired, provides a contrast to the neutral background of her designs with deep tones that can range from cinnamon to burnt sienna to a rich mocha. Occasionally, she will paint a red-dish slip—clay thinned to a liquid—on parts of her design for decorative effect.

Unlike the other female ceramists, Angélica Vásquez produces her clay pieces on her own, without the assistance of her children or other relatives, apart from her parents' help when she uses their kiln. She alone designs and molds her figures. Consequently, her ability to produce ceramics on a broad scale is more limited than the other artisans, the more so because she approaches her work with a distinctive artistic sensibility. Although there are some figural themes that she produces often, she tends not to duplicate her more detailed composi-

Nativity Angel
Angélica Vásquez

tions, preferring instead to create seven or eight truly original works a year. The act of creation in clay for her is as much a mental or meditative process as it is a manual one: "I find a quiet moment and I close my eyes, and in the dark, that's where I see my figures."

The wonderful array of ceramic designs on the shelves facing her reveals both her unique talents and her favorite motifs. Angels have always inspired her creativity: A piece that she has made as a wedding gift for a friend suggests her hope of divine blessing for the wedding couple, with bride and groom nestled protectively against celestial wings amidst an abundance of flowers. Clay images of strong women are displayed prominently, no doubt reflecting her own life experiences and hopes. A peasant woman stands authoritatively with machete in hand; a young girl, skirt swinging, jauntily balances a basin under her arm.

Angélica Vásquez's ceramic art is deeply rooted in Oaxacan popular culture. She has obviously continued to be enchanted with the spirits and myths of her grandmother's stories: "We are surrounded by a lot of magic, in the birds and all of the animals. Everything exists for something. I love to capture the folklore in clay." Many of her compositions are elaborate celebrations of Oaxacan traditions. One ceramic design on the shelf opposite her is a virtual collage of Oaxacan myths and reality: the symbols of corn and the Virgin of Guadalupe predominate, animal spirits and market women emerge from tiny niches, and mermaids frolic in the thick corded hair of a woman representing the sea.

The image of the mermaid—one of her favorite themes—threads together Angélica's passion for myth and her appreciation of spunk in women. In part, she says, she likes the visual beauty of the form itself: A recently finished piece has a mermaid leaning sensuously against a bed of coral adorned with sea anemones and other sea creatures; even Neptune is enchanted by her. But it is primarily "the audacity" of the mermaid, Angélica asserts, that attracts her. In Oaxacan legend, the mermaid is created when a young girl is transformed into one for disobeying her mother. But rather than viewing the mermaid as a symbol of disobedience, Angélica sees her as a celebration of freedom: a symbol of female daring in a society that values obedience in women.

She knows firsthand the debilitating effects of the conformity and the silence often imposed upon women in Mexican rural life. Even before her husband abandoned her, there were indications of harmful deceptions in her in-laws' home. She had continued to work in clay after her marriage, and her exceptional talent was quickly recognized: Her first award came at seventeen. As a dutiful daughter-in-law, Angélica always gave her finished pieces to her father-in-law—the *jefe* of the household—to handle for her. A chance congratulation at a social gathering, for winning first place in a national ceramic contest, stunned her: She'd had no idea that she had won the prize, or the money that came with it. "I started to feel that there were crooked things going on, but I couldn't figure out exactly what, because I wasn't allowed to speak with anyone."

It was after her husband left that she discovered that her father-in-law was giving her merely a fraction of the monies he received from selling her pieces—at a time when she and her children barely had enough to eat. She also learned that he had signed his own name to several of her pieces that had gone on to win major awards. The knowledge transformed her: "I think I was born in that moment, because I said, 'This is over.'" But her efforts to assert her independence by selling her work herself were thwarted by cultural expectations of female behavior. "A good woman is a submissive person, who does what she's told, especially if she is in her in-laws' house." Her well-connected father-in-law made sure that local shop owners would not buy her ceramics. She was forced to abandon the artisan work she loved, but she would not give up her dream of an independent life for herself and her children. "With each fall," she reflects, "I become stronger."

After trying her hand at just about everything to earn money in Atzompa, including making and selling tortillas and doing other people's wash, she found a job selling perfume and women's accessories in the city of Oaxaca. With grueling twelve-hour days, walking in the hot sun from office to office, she began to make enough to rebuild her life. And at the insistence of an American friend, who pressed her not to forsake her talent, Angélica also began to design again in clay. The same friend introduced her to a gallery owner who accepted her work without her father-in-law as intermediary. Almost immediately, her pieces garnered major awards. She soon was able to leave her retailing job to devote herself completely to clay, and her artistic gifts were soon rewarded: In the decade of the nineties she won a continual succession of honors—grand prizes, first places, special awards for innovation—in prestigious national and state competitions. Finally she was able to petition the municipal authorities in Atzompa for a plot of communal land upon which to build her own home. Six years ago she left her in-laws' compound. With her children and the new man in her life, an American, she made her move to the top of the hill.

The Enchanting Mermaid
Angélica Vásquez

There are still ways in which Angélica's determination to realize her potential as an individual and as an artisan is perceived as a challenge to cultural norms. Even the simple act of riding her bicycle rubs against the grain of ideas about appropriate behavior for women. But she endures the comments about being "a man," and continues to ride. And she insists on treating her children equally, encouraging her daughters, as well as her sons, to get an education. Her career is flourishing, with more awards, a number of exhibitions of her work, and a recent scholarship to study new ceramic techniques in the United States.

Outside her studio window, as she continues to work, she can see scarlet gladiolas and giant magenta dahlias. Vibrant pink bougainvillea gild the top of a small arbor, creating a refuge of repose from the hot sun. There are mangoes and guavas and papayas and pomegranates. Avocados are almost ready to be plucked. Tangerines and passion fruit soon will be. And there are hibiscus, more than two dozen kinds, everywhere. Her garden blooms.

Technique

Despite the distinctive talents and artistic interests of these artisans, all six share the common tasks and problems imposed by the process of working in clay. They all mark their days by the ritual of preparing the clay for molding—a never-ending process of drying out fresh clay, crushing it, weeding out debris, soaking it in water, then kneading it smooth. All rely on the same basic techniques associated with molding their creations entirely by hand, rejecting use of the treadle-driven potter's wheel. All use the simplest of tools to transform their artistic vision into tangible form: a small, worn piece of *cuero*—traditionally hide, but more often now felt, cut from a man's sombrero—to smooth and shape; a broken piece of gourd or tin to scrape and plane; a plant needle or thorn for detail. All utilize the open-air kiln so typical of the Mexican countryside: circular in shape, constructed of adobe and brick, open on top for stacking the pottery, with an opening below ground level for the fuel needed to build up the fire. And all must wage a constant battle against the elements of nature that threaten at any moment to undo their hard work: strong wind that can cause pieces to crack while drying or break in the kiln; rain seeping into a fired kiln that can destroy in a flash the work of previous weeks.

Angélica and her mother, Delfina, loading the kiln

Yet it is also striking the extent to which local village traditions affect the technical process of producing ceramics. Although Ocotlán and Atzompa are both nestled in the valley of Oaxaca not far from each other, there are significant differences in the ways in which the artisans in these two communities work. Some of the technical variations flow, of course, from the different types of ceramics that they produce. The Aguilar sisters fire their clay pieces once, then meticulously paint them to produce the polychromed figures for which they are famous. The natural earthenware compositions that Angélica Vásquez produces also require only a single firing, but her subtle hues come from the use of different colored clays before firing, not paint. Dolores Porras's use of glaze to produce her multicolored ceramic pots requires that she fires her ware twice, baking her colors into the clay during the second "cooking."

Dolores's husband and son unloading the kiln

When Dolores emphasizes that "we learn from our ancestors," she points to the distinctive historical roots of the clay inheritance each woman received from her family or community, a legacy that continues to distinguish the ceramic-making process. For instance, each town uses different types of clay, with obvious consequences for the preparation and firing of ceramic pieces.

In Santa María Atzompa, there are two primary sources of clay: *Barro liso*, literally, "smooth clay," which comes from the nearby village of San Lorenzo Cacaotepec; and *barro de golpear*, "hitting clay," which comes from Santa Catarina, also only a short distance away. *Barro liso* is black in color when fresh, but transforms to a creamy buff tone when fired. The "hitting clay," on the other hand, is a coarse, dirty white, gravelly substance that is never used alone. Once Atzompan artisans pulverize it by repeatedly hitting it with a club (hence its name), they mix it with *barro liso* to produce a stronger, less fragile clay called *barro áspero* or "rough clay." "Smooth clay" and the mixture that is "rough clay" are thus the two dominant clays used in Atzompa, and they serve very different purposes.

Josefina and family digging for clay

The strength of "rough clay" lends itself for use in making the large pots and cooking vessels for which Atzompa is known. Dolores Porras uses "rough clay" predominantly; Angélica Vásquez uses "rough clay" only for the bases of her compositions, which need to be strong enough to hold the elaborate display of intricate figures she applies to them. "Smooth clay" is more easily and delicately molded: Angélica uses it predominantly; Dolores uses "smooth" only for some of the decorative motifs that she applies to her vessels.

In contrast to the raw materials in Atzompa, the clay the Aguilar sisters use directly from the deposits in Ocotlán fires naturally to a reddish hue. It does not require mixing to fortify it, since the Aguilars do not produce cookware or large pots, and thus their ceramics do not need to withstand direct heat.

Josefina's son, Sergio, kneading the clay with his feet

Certain differences clearly flow from these variations in the nature of the clays. Preparing clay for use, laborious in any case, is particularly burdensome in Atzompa, since the "hitting clay" must be reduced to a powder before it can be mixed to produce "rough clay." All the usual debris—especially rocks and stones—must be carefully sifted out in a time-consuming process. Differences in the properties of the clay used may well explain the unusual method the Aguilar sisters use to massage the moistened clay in its final stages of preparation: feet—not hands as in Atzompa and elsewhere—are their instruments of choice for kneading. The "dance" performed to ensure the proper pliability of the clay has always been in the Aguilar family. Josefina remembers kneading the clay with her feet as a child, and this ritual may reflect family tradition, not the nature of the clay itself.

Certainly tradition explains the unique tools the women in

Dolores's *molde* and *volteador*

each community use to mold their figures. The Aguilar sisters use a distinctive mallet—the *azotador*—to pound the clay flat to begin to form their figures. Their mother had always used it to flatten the clay, and they have simply followed suit. Like Isaura before them, the sisters make the *azotador* themselves, molding and baking it from the very same clay they use for their art. In contrast, Dolores and Angélica in Atzompa always flatten the clay solely with their hands. Yet Atzompa too has its distinctive implements: the *molde* and the *volteador*. Used primarily by women like Dolores, who create pots and other large, rounded vessels, the *molde* is the circular earthenware disk used as a base on which to shape the clay; it balances and rotates on the *volteador*, typically spherical in shape, sometimes simply a flipped-over bowl. Both implements are made from baked "rough clay," and some women in Atzompa devote themselves exclusively to producing these special tools.

Perhaps the most striking difference in the ways in which these women produce their ceramics lies in the firing process and the preparation for it. Because of the different clays, the duration of firing time for the clay pieces differs sharply in the two communities. Angélica's pieces are fired for some three hours. Dolores also "cooks" her ware for three hours—sometimes a bit more—for each of the two firings necessary in her work. The ceramics of Ocotlán bake for more than double the time of these firings in Atzompa. Utilizing a much slower flame, each of the Aguilar sisters fires her pieces for eight to nine hours, often longer. Perhaps because of the shorter but more intense heat to which Atzompa ceramics are exposed, Dolores and Angélica need to warm their clay pieces in the heat of the sun for hours before they fire them in the kiln. The usual procedure for all six women is to dry their freshly molded pieces for several days indoors before firing. (The exact number of days depends on the weather; rain extends the drying period.) In Atzompa, putting the dried but cold clay pots or figures directly into the kiln virtually ensures that they will explode during firing. In Ocotlán, none of the Aguilars find it necessary to warm up their molded clay figures in the sun before firing them in the kiln.

Undoubtedly all of these artisans have been affected by the larger changes in their environment, as Oaxaca itself has changed, in some ways dramatically, over the last decades. Some of these changes have eased the artisan process, reflecting the introduction of new materials into the valley. The only major change Isaura's daughters have introduced into the craft they learned from her is the use of acrylic paint. Their mother used only aniline paint, harder to apply and less trustworthy in its results: it faded quickly and was easily stained by water.

But some of the ways in which Oaxaca has changed have made ceramic production more burdensome. Gone are the days when artisan families would gather their own wood in the countryside. Nowadays one must buy the wood. Guillermina Aguilar notes, "When we used to gather it ourselves, there was firewood close by. Now it is farther away, more expensive, and very scarce." Deforestation has taken its toll, adding to the pressures the artisans face daily as they create their art.

Josefina's Tools
Counterclockwise from left: *Apaxtle* with water; *azotador*; piece of tin to cut the clay; dried maguey leaf with thorn; clay; ice pick for etching lines; larger maguey leaf with thorn

Inspiration

As the art of the people, folk art is always deeply rooted in popular culture. These women's ceramics demonstrate that vividly. For all six women, the images and motifs that inspire their work envelop their daily worlds. Whether they are worshipping in church, joining the celebration at a family wedding, or simply weaving through the colorful and aromatic passageways of the market, they are surrounded by customs and beliefs that spark the imagination. The astonishingly rich cultural world of Oaxaca—and all of Mexico—offers a limitless source of creativity for their popular art.

Frida
Concepción Aguilar
Cactus
Jorge Sánchez Ruiz,
Concepción's husband

Although they draw upon tradition and custom as a source of inspiration, these artisans do more than reproduce the dominant symbols of their culture repetitively in their ceramics. While they use some timeless and unchanging techniques, their work shows endless thematic innovation. In this sense, the clay compositions of these six women parallel the remarkable adaptiveness of Oaxacans. Responding to the new global influences today, as they did to the Spanish Conquest half a millennium ago and the infusion of American styles and gadgets in this century, Oaxacans allow in the new, transforming it to make it their own.

The ceramists similarly absorb and transform—"Oaxacanize"—the suggestive influences that originate beyond their state. The current popularity of Frida Kahlo images made by the Aguilar sisters is a case in point. All have adapted Kahlo's arresting self-portraits to the style of their own figural ceramics so successfully that their clay Fridas appear the embodiment of Oaxacan womanhood. Sometimes the suggestions of outsiders, like the U.S. shop owner with a fascination for insects, may seem alien, but even here Concepción Aguilar found a way to incorporate clay insects into a traditional motif so that they appear a typical part of Oaxacan lore. These artisans, then, draw upon the lush imagery and the abundant variety of Oaxacan customs, but they creatively adapt and renew these traditions as well.

The most common themes they use derive from the major elements of popular culture in Oaxaca. Myths and legends, intertwining the fantastic and the real, are important sources of inspiration. Religion, and the festival calendar it generates, also strongly influences their work. Other celebratory events and rituals, whether community-wide celebrations or family ceremonies, provide visual stimuli for art as much as they impart festivity into lives too often marked by struggle and pain. Even ordinary daily routine—never devoid of color and grace in Oaxaca—inspires each of these women to create artistry in clay.

Myths and Legends

The rich folklore of Oaxaca and the oral tradition on which it is based produce a sumptuous bounty upon which the creative imaginations of these women can feast. All six women heard myths and legends when they were very young at their grandmothers' side. The tales were a significant part of their education, orienting them, as young children, to both the magic and the dangers of Oaxacan life. As adults, they have continued to honor these legends, conveying them to their children and relating them through their art.

The continuing vitality of these suggestive legends is a fertile source of inspiration for the artisans' work in clay. At the same time, the very power of these myths also reveals something significant about the defining cultural characteristics of worldview and belief in Oaxaca. For these women, the myths and legends are not fables to be relegated to some fictional shelf. Mythic figures are fabulous and real at the same time. This is, perhaps, the essence of what magical realism in Latin America—amply reflected in these women's ceramics—is all about.

One of the most prevalent legends, which all six women draw upon frequently in their art, embodies important lessons about appropriate behavior for girls. The *sirena* or mermaid motif pervades Mexican folk art, but in Oaxaca, mermaids have their own distinct lore. Josefina Aguilar remembers hearing from her grandmother about a young woman who always went to bathe by the banks of the river. The girl's mother would scold her for her frequent trips to the river when there was no need to get water. One day the girl went to bathe even though her mother expressly forbade it. According to Angélica Vásquez, "When she decided to come out of the river and return home, she couldn't because all of her body that was in the water had become scaled like a fish. She had become half human and half fish." Angélica adds that the mermaid consoled herself with a guitar— the only diversion she was now allowed—"so she could sing of her sadness and melancholy."

As Guillermina Aguilar reconciles the tale with her own religious faith—"it was already going to happen by God's will"—she too expresses her belief in its legitimacy. "There are still places the mermaid inhabits, even though she has lived for hundreds of years already." Guillermina notes that a mermaid's presence

Mermaid

Josefina Aguilar

Mermaids

Irene Aguilar

Mermaids

Angélica Vásquez

Mermaid Platter

Dolores Porras

Mermaid Plate

Josefina Aguilar

Mermaids

Josefina Aguilar

can be seen "in the swirls of water she makes when she comes," although "you have to be very lucky to see her." All three women agree that the best chance to glimpse her is on the 24th of June—the feast day of San Juan—when she comes out to sing and comb her hair by the banks of the river. Angélica explains that in the very moment the girl was transformed into a mermaid, her hair grew long enough to cover her naked body. Consequently, Oaxacan women honor the mermaid by cutting their hair on June 24. (In Atzompa, custom dictates that it is doubly special if a man cuts the woman's hair; some even believe it is important to plant the hair trimmings in moist earth. In Ocotlán, women trim their own hair on that day in the belief that it will then grow very quickly.)

Beliefs about the magical relationship between humans and animals are widespread in the valley of Oaxaca and throughout Mexico. The special powers of animals over the direction of human life appear in many local myths, which sometimes inexplicably resonate more strongly in some communities than in others close by. The vibrancy of traditional beliefs about the *nahual* in Atzompa is a case in point. The *nahual* is an animal protector—a guardian spirit—that an individual acquires at birth. Teodora Blanco popularized the belief about *nahuales* through her creative use of them in clay. Befitting their shared Atzompan roots, Angélica Vásquez imaginatively continues the use of this beguiling imagery in her own ceramic work, reflecting the same fascination with her heritage and the richness with which it can be translated into clay.

"They say," Angélica explains, "that when a woman was going to give birth, the couple would burn a special kind of wood that would make white ash." After the woman gave birth, the couple would take both the placenta and the white ash and put them on the ground where two paths cross—usually somewhere in the mountains—and then hide and watch. "The first animal that passed, leaving its prints in the ash, that was the animal that would protect you for the rest of your life."

La Matlacihua
Angélica Vásquez

Sometimes, "because parents want the best for their children," couples would wait for a few animals to pass by, selecting as the child's *nahual* the one whose characteristics they most favored—fleetness or bravery, for example—for their child. Although Atzompan couples no longer select *nahuales* for their children, the underlying beliefs still have power in the community.

Other versions of *nahual* beliefs in the valley do not take the benign form emphasized in Atzompa. The work of Teodora Blanco and Angélica Vásquez draws inspiration from the positive connections between humans and their animal spirits: the role played by the *nahual* as guardian and protector. Yet the darker side to the *nahual* myth may explain why the Aguilar sisters in Ocotlán rarely use this imagery in their work. Guillermina notes how burdensome and difficult the *nahual* tale can be: If the animal that is one's guardian spirit is harmed or killed, then one experiences the same injury or death. Her great uncle died when his *nahual*, a wolf, was killed. For this reason, Jesús Aguilar would not allow his own family to take up the custom of identifying a child with a *nahual*, though he himself had one. ("I believe it was a buzzard," Guillermina adds. "Imagine that! When my father was nervous, my grandmother said it was because his buzzard had lost its way to the place where it slept.") Moreover, some legends emphasize directly how threatening animals can be: Tradition also has it that witches often transform themselves into animals to do harm to their enemies. These more troublesome myths rarely find their way into clay.

While all six ceramists, like most Oaxacans, believe deeply in other popular legends, it is Angélica Vásquez especially whose work most often draws directly from them. Her sheer delight in Oaxacan folklore—"I just love these tales!"—and the creative exhilaration she derives from it continually stimulate her art. Two of the most popular legends that she represents in clay are *La Matlacihua* and *La Llorona*.

The myth of *La Matlacihua* tells of a seductive beauty who lures men down lonely paths at night and then swiftly transforms into a demon to do them harm. As

Market Woman
with her *Nahuales*
Angélica Vásquez

legend has it, Angélica explains, not all men are her targets: "The men who are punished are not clean. That is to say, they are not true to their wives." Josefina Aguilar notes that *La Matlacihua* "shows herself the most to men who like women a lot." Her sister Concepción adds, "She does harm to men because they harm their wives."

All of the artisans know someone who has had a close encounter with this dangerous seductress. Dolores Porras's husband, Alfredo, remembers seeing her late one night on his way home, but he fortunately recognized her real nature: when he looked down, "she had no feet." Dolores remembers her father's brush with danger when she walked with him one evening and they met a strangely beautiful woman. When her father tipped his hat to her, "we saw that she didn't have feet like us. They were like horse hooves or a donkey's. We got scared and the woman disappeared. And we left with fear." Josefina Aguilar also relates the experience of male relatives who were entrapped by *La Matlacihua*. "They say it's like a ghost, a wind. They follow her and they get covered with thorns, tearing up their clothes."

Because Angélica Vásquez's childhood home was on the edge of town—"where they say she walks"—she has vivid memories of late-night cries for help. "Near where we lived, three fields away, there was some barbed wire and that's where these men would get entangled, yelling." Sometimes there were desperate pleas right at her front door, when someone would cry, "Please help me. My name is so-and-so and I want to get back to my house because *La Matlacihua* took me." Angélica can still recall her fright. "Because we were children, we would get scared. They would come in with their clothes all dirty, with thorns in their hands, all messed up."

Perhaps the intensity with which she recalls these childhood feelings fuels her creative use of this legend in clay. One of her pieces in particular conveys the complex metamorphosis involved in the tale: *La Matlacihua*'s transformation from beautiful seductress into a decaying demon—monsters forming from her side—and her final emergence as Death, calling for her male victims.

La Llorona, The Weeping Woman, is another of the renowned Mexican myths that Angélica represents in clay. Although many versions of this classic circulate throughout Mexico (indeed, it has now rooted widely in the U.S. as well), the basic story relates the tragedy of a woman whose despair drove her to kill her own children. For punishment, she wanders forever, weeping, in search of them.

Angélica describes the source of *La Llorona*'s desperation: "She was a pretty woman who had children, but her husband tricked her. He abandoned her for another woman and she thought she had no reason to live. Feeling so insulted, so sad, so desperate, she thought about dying, but she worried that if she died, her

children would suffer alone. So her solution was to kill them. In the moment she committed the evil deed, she began to regret it. But there was nothing she could do. Her children were dead and so she committed suicide. Instead of dying, she was forced to wander." Angélica concludes the Oaxacan variant of the tale: "They say that she goes flying around the valley. They say that she suffers and that she goes around crying in all sorts of places in search of her children."

In her design, Angélica Vásquez depicts all the elements of this tale of a mother's suffering for her unpardonable sin. The hand of Death extends to receive the murdered children splattered with blood. On one side of the composition, the husband sneaks away with his suitcase, a symbol of his wandering ways that set the tragedy in motion. Angélica tucks a poisonous viper nearby, representing the woman who stole *La Llorona*'s husband. Demons bite the Weeping Woman's arm, tokens of her giving in to evil. A howling coyote—Angélica's favorite Atzompan symbol of bad luck—completes her rendition of the tale.

La Llorona:
The Weeping Woman
Angélica Vásquez

Religion

While Oaxacan myths and legends continually animate their artistry, these ceramists' deep religious faith infuses both their daily lives and their art. Dolores Porras expresses the intimate presence of religion in her life: "During every moment we say the name of God as we go to work, so that everything comes out well." Concepción Aguilar, whose religious images in clay shine with faith, reveals her own spiritual roots: "When one is going through life, when one suffers, one knows that she needs God for many things." Her sister Irene's gratitude for the immediacy of God in her life knows no bounds: "My whole life would not be enough to thank God for everything He has given me." Guillermina Aguilar, the embodiment of religious devotion, similarly reflects on the seeds of her piety: "I have received from Our Lord very great and wonderful responses. He has given me a lot, too much." She recalls that the first time she flew in a plane she knew no fear because "I was closer to God."

San José y la Virgen de los Dolores, **Saint Joseph and the Virgin of Sorrows**
Josefina Aguilar

One cannot emphasize enough the cultural and social importance of religion in Oaxaca, as well as its ritual, as a continuing source of inspiration for these women's art. The Catholicism implanted by the Spanish Conquest, itself transformed by its merging with indigenous beliefs, pervades community life. Religion is everywhere, not merely confined to the pious exercise of ritual in church. Home altars imbue households with religious sentiment. Frequent religious processions wind through village streets, creating bonds among villagers. The many celebrations of saints provide opportunities for festivity in both individual and community routines.

There has always been a fertile connection between religion and art throughout Latin America. In Oaxaca, popular art is intimately linked to religious belief. With ceramics, that linkage often takes the direct form of clay incense burners and candlesticks that adorn altars. For these six women artisans, the images of their piety permeate their clay designs. While saints and nativity scenes recur in their work, the myriad Virgins that inhabit the Mexican Catholic landscape seem to have especially captured their hearts.

The enchantment with these Virgins reflects their symbolic meaning as beacons of hope. Josefina Aguilar perhaps best explains the attraction when she notes the maternal nourishment that homage to these sacred icons provides: "The Virgin gives us consolation, as if she were a mother." The Virgin also facilitates a connection between faith and miracles that perpetuates her veneration. Again Josefina captures well the underlying belief: "The thing is, it depends on what your faith is.

Three Virgins
opposite, from left to right:
La Virgen del Rosario, **The Virgin of the Rosary;** *La Virgen del Sagrado Corazón de Jesús,* **The Virgin of the Sacred Heart of Jesus;** *La Virgen de Guadalupe,* **The Virgin of Guadalupe**
Concepción Aguilar

La Virgen de Guadalupe:
The Virgin of Guadalupe
Dolores Porras

Miracle at Tepeyac
Angélica Vásquez

If you have faith in the *Virgen de Juquila* or *de la Soledad* or *de Guadalupe*, then she will have the power to help you, to comfort you." The Virgin thus sustains the miraculous reality in which all six believe. This belief in the real possibility of miracles through faith inspires the artisans' frequent pilgrimages to the Virgins' sacred sites. It also stimulates the continuing desire to recreate these venerable images in clay. The three Virgins that Josefina Aguilar mentions—the Virgin of Guadalupe, the Virgin of Solitude, and the Virgin of Juquila—have special importance for these artisans, as they do for all Oaxacans.

Religion and myth merge in the tale of the Virgin of Guadalupe, the patron saint of Mexico. Soon after the Spanish Conquest, this dark-skinned Virgin appeared before a poor Indian, Juan Diego, on the Hill of Tepeyac, the very site where a temple to the Aztec goddess, Tonantzin, had stood before. Guillermina Aguilar relates how the Virgin asked the boy to seek out the bishop, "so that all would see that she was the Virgin, that she was the mother of God." Juan Diego went to tell of the Virgin's miraculous appearance, but as he feared, no one believed him. Angélica Vásquez continues the well-known story. "Juan Diego returned again to the Virgin telling her they asked for proof. She said, 'My son, this is the proof that I give you, and take it to the priest so he'll see you are not a liar and that I want a church built for me here.' In that moment, a garden full of roses and birds appeared. The Virgin told him, 'Cut all the roses you want and take them.'" When Juan Diego opened his cloak before the bishop to reveal his armload of flowers, there were none. Instead, the image of the Virgin was miraculously imprinted on the cloth of his cloak.

The shrine built in Mexico City on the site of the Virgin of Guadalupe's miraculous appearance in 1531 remains the most sacred in the nation, befitting "the Queen of Mexico," the country's first saint. Like the hundreds of thousands of other Mexican pilgrims who seek solace in honoring her, all six of these artists venerate her awesome power. Josefina Aguilar reflects the experience of most: "I have asked her for many things and she has granted me them. There are times when a child is sick, or when you are sick, or you have a broken foot or something. You go to ask her that you get better and you do. Or sometimes you find

yourself without money, and you go cry to the Virgin that you need work, and the Virgin comes through."

Concepción Aguilar expresses in a similar way her faith in the miraculous powers of the *Virgen de la Soledad*, the Virgin of Solitude: "I love the Virgin of Solitude very much. I have always gone there to where she is. I pray to her that there never be a lack of work and there never has been." This local Virgin, the

The Hill of Tepeyac
Josefina Aguilar

Nativity
Angélica Vásquez

Three Wise Men
Concepción Aguilar

opposite:
Tree of Life
Guillermina Aguilar

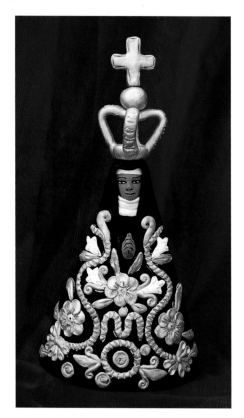

La Virgen de la Soledad:
The Virgin of Solitude
Irene Aguilar

La Virgen de Juquila:
The Virgin of Juquila
Irene Aguilar

patroness of the capital city of Oaxaca de Juárez, appeared almost a century after the Virgin of Guadalupe when a muleteer in Oaxaca realized he was traveling with an extra mule. When the mysterious mule suddenly died, a statue of the exquisite Virgin was found in the bags slung on his back. To honor her, a magnificent baroque church was built in the seventeenth century on the exact site of her astonishing appearance. The beautiful statue still remains encased in glass inside the church, and it is here that Oaxacans come to revere her. While all six ceramists pay homage to her, the Virgin of Solitude's elegant dress—black velvet lavishly embroidered with gold and silver—lends itself to representation in the ceramic style of the Aguilar sisters, whose painted figures capture the richness of the Virgin's lovely image.

Perhaps the most intriguing Virgin in Oaxaca is the Thumbelina-sized Virgin from Santa Catarina Juquila. Found in the mountains of Oaxaca after the Conquest, the Virgin had a temple constructed in her honor. "But then there was a fire," Angélica Vásquez explains, "and the whole church burned down."

The Virgin, however, remained unharmed, only slightly tinged by smoke. "Since then," Angélica continues, "the Virgin of Juquila is greatly venerated because people believe that there was a miracle when she was left in the middle of the ashes of the great fire."

This diminutive Virgin has, these six women agree, great powers. All would concur with Concepción Aguilar's assessment that "her size is very small, but her miracles are very big." Each artisan has her own special recollection of the wondrous favors this Virgin has bestowed upon her family. Dolores Porras, for example, has made seven pilgrimages to seek her favor, and after each, the Virgin has granted her request. She attributes her home, her success as a ceramist, and even the trees in her patio to the Virgin of Juquila's miraculous generosity.

The trip to honor the Virgin, from either Atzompa or Ocotlán, is not an easy one. For Josefina Aguilar and her family, it entails about four days of walking each way. But, as Josefina explains, one goes prepared. "You buy new sandals and you take a package of tortillas, coffee, sugar, that's all, so at night when you stay in the fields you make your coffee and eat some tortillas and you keep walking day and night." The effort expended to show one's faith in the Virgin earns an ample reward because of the miracles she has the power to create. For Josefina, the Virgin of Juquila has responded to all her heartfelt pleas. "Whatever you ask her for, she gives you. The first time I went, she granted me the wish for my husband and then later when we both went, I asked her to be able to buy my house and I bought the house. Then later we went and I asked her that we would have a lot of work and that tourists would come and my work would sell." The Virgin of Juquila even responded to one of Josefina's most fervent longings: After giving birth to six sons, she and José wanted a girl, "and she granted us that."

Like her younger sisters, Guillermina Aguilar believes very deeply in the Virgin of Juquila, "ever since my grandmother transmitted this message of the Virgin to us." Her faith too has been abundantly rewarded. When she and her husband, Leopoldo, longed to buy their first home, they went to ask her for it "and just as we asked, the Virgin gave it to us." When they had the opportunity to move to the main road, near Josefina, they again sought help from the Virgin to be able to buy the land—and again she granted their request. Guillermina's abiding faith in the Virgin of Juquila necessitates more than an occasional pilgrimage to pay her homage: "We need to go every year. Every year my children go by bicycle, walking, or in a car, or however they can. But it is necessary to see the Virgin."

Five Virgins
clockwise from top left: *La Virgen de San Juan de los Lagos*, The Virgin of San Juan of the Lakes; *La Virgen de Covadonga*, The Virgin of Covadonga; *La Virgen de la Asunción*, The Virgin of the Assumption; *La Virgen del Rosario*, The Virgin of the Rosary; *La Virgen del Carmen*, The Virgin of Carmen
Josefina Aguilar

Celebrations

For all Oaxacans, December is a particularly festive month, not only because of *La Navidad* (Christmas), but also because it marks the miraculous appearances of all three Virgins: the Virgin of Guadalupe on the twelfth, the Virgin of Solitude on the eighteenth, and the Virgin of Juquila on the eighth. Elaborate festivities in their honor take place which sparkle with the spirit of exuberance for which Mexico is renowned. Oaxacans, in particular, take their celebrations seriously; the ceremony surrounding these homages to the Virgin, like all Oaxacan celebrations, offers a cornucopia of color and artistry. Music and fireworks provide the background to a bounty of celebratory foods: steamed tamales, their fragrant fillings seeping out of their banana leaf or corn husk wrappings; rich *moles*, the complex Mexican sauces made with chilies, spices, nuts, and, in Oaxaca, unsweetened chocolate; thick *atoles*, the sweet, gruel-like pre-Columbian drink served on special occasions. Processions snake through community streets, girls garbed traditionally in vibrantly embroidered cotton, their heads balancing baskets filled with intricate floral bouquets—themselves works of popular art—laugh and rush to keep up, giant puppets prance in their midst. Oaxacan fiestas are a feast for the senses, a wonderful explosion of sound, taste, and movement.

opposite:
Viva la Revolución
Josefina Aguilar

Monos de Calenda:
Festival puppets
Concepción Aguilar

These rituals of celebration fill the Oaxacan calendar with ceremony. In both Santa María Atzompa and Ocotlán de Morelos, virtually every month of the year is the occasion for one festival or another. The importance of these celebrations is woven into the very fabric of community life. For villagers, the rhythm of the year takes the shape of the festival calendar; the passage of time is measured by the celebrations past and the ceremonies to come. For these ceramists, the festivities represent visual banquets to savor, constant sources of nourishment for their designs in clay.

Most community celebrations are predominantly, but not exclusively, religious. The holy days of the Catholic Church and homages to cherished saints serve as the mainstay of the celebratory calendar. The sacred, solemn days of *Semana Santa* (Holy Week) in spring, in particular, have great spiritual importance in both

Musicians
Irene Aguilar

communities. Some ceremonies are historically linked to the agricultural cycle, expressing Oaxacan peasant farmers' traditional fears and hopes about enough water, plentiful harvests, and healthy animals. In early May, on the Day of the Holy Cross, for example, wells are blessed and adorned with flowers in both Atzompa and Ocotlán. During planting season in May and June, Oaxacans make appeals to saints such as San Juan, San Pedro, and San Pablo to ensure sufficient water and good crops. In the fall, both communities honor San Lucas, the patron of animals, by draping the necks of their cows and bulls with necklaces of flowers or apples.

Some days of ceremony are completely secular. National celebrations tied to important events or figures in Mexican history—like Mexico's Independence, the Mexican Revolution, or heroes like Benito Juárez, Oaxaca's revered native son— imbue the festivities with patriotic fervor. Other secular celebrations (like Mother's Day and the Day of Love and Friendship on February 14th) reflect international trends and the impact of more recent global and commercial influences.

Some celebrations are distinctively and importantly local, helping to forge strong bonds of identity between individuals and their community. Both Atzompa and Ocotlán have their own patron saints: *La Virgen de la Asunción* in Atzompa, *Santo Domingo de Guzmán* in Ocotlán. The week-long jubilees in their honor each August— filled with music, dance, and fireworks—are among the most important of the year. Other local festivals evolved out of special circumstance or custom: Atzompa has a February celebration honoring its own Saint of the Choir; Ocotlán has its May festivals of spring, which include the selection of a local Queen (Josefina and José's daughter, Leticia, was chosen a while back). And Ocotlán holds its own version of *Lunes del Cerro*—Monday on the Hill, the famous July festival that the capital city of Oaxaca celebrates in grand fashion, when dancers from the seven regions of the state gather in traditional dress to regale each other with indigenous regional dances. Also known by its Zapotec name, *Guelaguetza*, this quintessentially Oaxacan fiesta depicts the ritual of reciprocity or mutual exchange so characteristic of Oaxacan culture.

La Guelaguetza
Concepción Aguilar

Las Chinas Oaxaqueñas:
Festival Dancers
Guillermina Aguilar

Celebrations, however, should not thought of as mere parties, just affording people the opportunity for merrymaking and jubilation. Quite the contrary. For Oaxacans, these represent serious business. Beneath the revelry and ritual lie multiple hidden agendas. There is the serious matter of courtship: In a social world where girls' mobility is restricted and they are closely watched, community celebrations provide the only opportunity, apart from school, where young people have the freedom to eye each other and socialize.

Dancers
Dolores Porras

There is the serious business of network-building: In communities where bonds of friendship form the primary safety net of support, festivals provide an important means of solidifying existing relationships and creating new ones. Irene Aguilar explains the intricate rules of obligation and reward that lie just beneath the social surface: "If they invite me, I have to go, because I now owe that person a visit. It's a *guelaguetza*, a gift, that you take—some beer or soda or animals. But when I have a celebration, he has to return what I have lent him." The social record of one's obligations is often formally kept: for Irene, her notebook records "what comes in and what goes out." She can then keep the record straight: "I can go and give him what he lent me and what I now have to give him." In an economic world marked by scarcity, it is a creative system of mutual aid.

There is too, of course, the "serious" business, in the midst of hard lives, of simply having fun. The sheer humor and gaiety of the customs surrounding important life-cycle celebrations, such as weddings, elicit irrepressible laughter from the participants as much as they inspire impressive clay figures from these artisan

Wedding Angel
Angélica Vásquez

women. The tradition in Ocotlán, for example, of *la despedida de soltera* — the good-bye party for the bride-to-be, which takes place a week before the wedding — includes "the taking of the turkey." The groom's family bedecks two turkeys in full wedding dress and takes the "bride" and "groom" (with a cigar proudly dangling from his beak) in a basket, along with tortillas, *mole*, chocolate, beer, and firecrackers—even firewood to cook the meal—to the bride's house. In Atzompa, where a wedding becomes, in Angélica Vásquez's words, "a fiesta in capital letters," the entire bridal cortege winds its way through town carrying food, drink, and gifts for the bride. Here villagers adorn the ceremonial turkeys with necklaces of jewel-toned bougainvillea, and all the participants, turkeys included, dance through the streets as they make their way to the bride's home.

One of the most important celebrations in Atzompa and Ocotlán, the uniquely Mexican ritual of *el Día de los Muertos*, the Day of the Dead, commemorates the souls of the dead. For these six women, like all Mexicans, the ceremonies that take place at graveside and at home offer cherished opportunities to honor loved ones. As folk artists, Angélica, Dolores, and the Aguilar sisters respond to the increasing international interest in the events and motifs associated with *Muertos* in their own inspired experimentation with Day of the Dead themes in clay.

Death Selling Flowers
Concepción Aguilar

In Oaxaca, *el Día de los Muertos* takes on special significance, as extensive preparations for the two days of ceremony on November 1 and November 2 (the Catholic All Saints' Day and All Souls' Day) begin weeks before. By October 31, markets overflow with the candles, flowers, incense, and celebratory foods people seek. It is often a very pressured—and costly—time, as people prepare elaborately for the returning souls, "because," as Angélica Vásquez explains, "their loved ones only come to visit once a year."

In homes, the returning souls of the dead find an altar laden with what they especially fancied in life. Once the souls arrive ("they say that they come at dawn," Concepción Aguilar notes), they partake of the bounty offered them and can then return to their graves knowing

that they have not been forgotten. For Guillermina Aguilar and others like her, "this is the grandest thing I do every year." Stories abound in both Atzompa and Ocotlán of the catastrophic consequences when souls arrive to find that no altar awaits them: Wounded and distraught, these souls make their way back to the grave, howling because of their neglect. "That's why my grandmother would say," Angélica comments, "'Rain or thunder, you are going to put up your altar.'"

Traditionally, the first souls to arrive are those of "the little angels"—children who have died. Since the experience of losing a child is so pervasive among Oaxacan women (in this group of six, Dolores, Guillermina, Concepción, and Angélica have all experienced the loss of a child), November 1—*el Día de los Angelitos*, the Day of the Little Angels—is particularly special because it is dedicated to honoring them. Sweets, rather than spicy foods, are set out on altars conveniently placed for children, low to the ground. November 2, the actual *Día de los Muertos*, honors *los muertos grandes*, the adult dead, with the special food, drink, and objects that these souls loved in life placed on altars for their pleasure. As Josefina Aguilar explains, "You put out on your altar everything that they liked. For example, if he liked to drink, then you have to put out his bottle; if he smoked, his cigarettes." She remembers that after her father's death, her family set out even his musket—Jesús Aguilar loved hunting—for his soul's return.

Muertos
Irene Aguilar

The sheer beauty of the spectacle of these ceremonies includes an abundance of bright yellow marigold flowers, a soft radiance of glimmering candles, and spirals of smoky haze from the *copal* incense, which has burned on altars in Mexico for centuries. Petals from the marigolds, or *cempasúchil*, the traditional flower of the dead, mark the path from grave to home, so the souls, particularly of children, do not get lost. The altars, crammed lushly with *mole*, *tamales*, *pan de muertos* (the special bread for the Day of the Dead), tortillas, chocolate, and ripe fruit, burst

Come Dance with Me
Angélica Vásquez

with color and aroma, helping to create the celebratory mood. No wonder the Day of the Dead offers such inspiration for these artisans of clay.

opposite:

Las Catrinas
Josefina Aguilar

The Mexican attitude toward death is at once deeply spiritual, respectful, joyful, and irreverent. The playfulness appears particularly in folk art, where death has become a favorite theme. The images of skulls, skeletons, and coffins have been increasingly prominent in popular art, including in edible form, with elaborately crafted sugar skulls and *pan de muertos* that are creative works of art. The humor inherent in these visions draws a direct line of lineage to the celebrated prints of José Guadalupe Posada, the famous turn-of-the-century engraver whose skeletons frolic, mock, and cavort shamelessly. Josefina Aguilar appropriates one of Posada's most popular images, that of *La Catrina*, the fashionable skeleton in elegant dress, and her rendition of this figure shows how festively the symbols of Mexican celebrations can be transformed into clay.

Funeral
Irene Aguilar

Everyday Events

Besides the drama and pomp of Mexican celebrations, the color and ceremony of everyday life in Oaxaca provide ample inspiration for artful designs in clay. Ordinary daily routine—and the vivid scenes of human life derived from it—kindle creative imaginations as much as the formal ritual of the festival calendar. The market, for example, the teeming center of Oaxacan community life, is a continually changing canvas of form and figure. Exquisitely stacked mounds of food—shiny green jalapeño chilies or the brilliant orange zucchini blossoms or snowy piles of onions—represent compositions of art in their own right. Perhaps because it is so important in the lives of women, the market and its motifs are prominent themes in the work of all these ceramists. Market women, Doña Isaura Alcántara's favorite theme, emerge in clay as stately matrons marching to and fro, proudly hawking their wares.

The small rituals of life—tiny snatches of scenes unfolding daily in each community—also afford images that can be captured in clay: a moment of intimacy in a café, time taken to rest on a park bench, a dazed slouch in a chair from one drink too many. And then there are the timeless rites of passage between birth and death that touch us all. These six talented artisans energize and transform clay to produce scenes of the ordinary and eternal events of life, from baptisms to funerals and all the human drama in between.

opposite:
Market Woman Selling Pottery
Guillermina Aguilar

After the Celebration
Josefina Aguilar

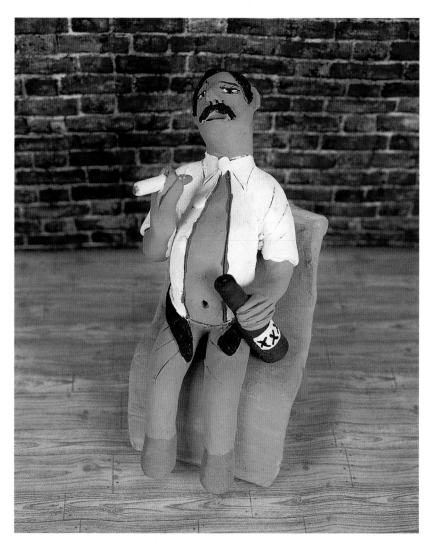

Women Cooking
Irene Aguilar

Market Women
Josefina Aguilar

opposite:
Market Woman
Dolores Porras

Market Women
Irene Aguilar

At the Park
Josefina Aguilar

opposite:
The Café
Angélica Vásquez

Family

While the clay artistry that each woman produces flows uniquely from her individual talents, all of these artisans are sustained in important ways by family. Profoundly rooted in Mexican culture, family involves traditions of deep respect for parents and loving appreciation of children. The meaning of family takes on special economic and social significance in rural Mexico, where scarce resources do not guarantee even a marginal existence. In the midst of continual economic struggle, family members usually take responsibility to assure the survival of the family unit, contributing unselfishly to its sustenance. Like most Oaxacan mothers, these six women can count on the unstinting support of their children, who are always regarded as a substantial resource. (Dolores Porras and Guillermina Aguilar have nine children apiece, Josefina Aguilar has eight, Angélica Vásquez four, Irene Aguilar and Concepción Aguilar three each.) Traditions, like those whereby sons begin their married lives still under their parents' roof, further serve to bind the Oaxacan home into an intensely close-knit whole. In the countryside, family becomes one's ultimate weapon for survival.

Flower Girls
Estela Sánchez de Cruz,
Concepción's daughter

For women artisans, the support of family takes on added meaning. The particular demands of their work—and their special vulnerabilities as women in Oaxacan society—mean that they often must depend on family members to complete various tasks. Oaxacan women, for example, rarely have had the opportunity for much schooling. Four of these women, in fact, never attended school at all. Only Angélica Vásquez completed primary school. Illiteracy always brings with it powerlessness; for artisans who need to communicate with clients on a regular basis, inability to read and write brings with it a need to depend on others.

Many aspects of the artisanal process are premised on cultural ideas about what is, and what is not, appropriate work for women. In both Ocotlán and Atzompa, most believe that it is men's work to prepare the clay, gather the firewood, fire the kiln,

Concepción Aguilar
working with her daughter
Estela and her son-in-law
Gustavo

above left:
**Self Portrait with
My family**
Josefina Aguilar

above right:
**Tribute to My Mother,
Josefina Aguilar**
Demetrio García Aguilar

and transport or ship the finished ceramics to their destination. Women artisans, therefore, customarily depend on their partners and sons to accomplish these tasks; those who are single or without sons face a challenge.

Because of family, these artisan women can expand their ceramic production. With spouses and children to help with painting or glazing, they can focus their creative energies on generating ideas and molding their designs, and can

Ladies of the Night
Julian García Aguilar,
Guillermina's son

opposite:
**Saint Michael,
Slayer of Dragons**
Julian García Aguilar

Fridas
Guadalupe García de González, Guillermina's daughter

Juan Carlos Z. Aguilar, Irene Aguilar's son

opposite:
Magic Hands
Juan Carlos Z. Aguilar

produce enough to meet demand and maintain the family. (Angélica Vásquez is the only ceramist of the six to work entirely on her own and consequently, her ceramic production is more limited than the others.)

One of the most striking aspects of family help is the underlying democracy of attitudes about who can create popular art. In contrast to elitist views in other cultures, which hold artistic talent as rare, innate, or the product of specialized training, these Oaxacan popular artists believe fervently that good folk art comes from caring hearts. Husbands and children—even daughters-in-law or sons-in-law who recently have become members of the family—can create marvelous ceramics regardless of prior experience or inborn aptitude.

Many of the adult children of these six women choose to work themselves as ceramists, and the inheritance of clay produces the same advantages for them that it worked in their mothers' lives. No doubt growing up in artisan house-

holds whose very rhythm is determined by pottery has a great effect. Young children play at their mother's knee, toying with the clay while their mothers mold. They spend their childhoods watching and listening in courtyards with freshly dug clay drying, the kiln firing, and tourists mulling over what to buy. While children growing up are expected to pitch in and help with family chores—which do revolve around clay—they are nonetheless prompted to do as adults what interests them most. Children who show a serious interest in clay are encouraged to pursue it, and usually by their early teen years are working long hours, under their mothers' watchful eyes, to develop their craft. Certainly the economic advantage of pursuing artisan work matters here: in Oaxaca, with few job opportunities and a usual wage of less than three dollars per day, the magic of clay also has its economic lure.

The talent and skill reflected in the ceramics created by these women's children are astonishing. Whether these gifts result from their familiarity and exposure to the craft, their own hard effort, or their mothers' loving instruction, this group of young ceramists clearly represent the next generation of Oaxacan artists in clay. Several are rapidly developing their own national and international reputations as folk artists, not merely carrying forward the ceramic traditions they have inherited, but creatively innovating and transforming them as well.

Josefina Aguilar's son, Demetrio García Aguilar, has already garnered numerous awards for his finely-sculptured compositions in clay. Now thirty-one, Demetrio began making and selling his own small figures when he was fourteen. The pieces he produces are intricate works of art, with a distinctive artistic level of concern. He has created his own unusual style of painting, mixing colors himself to achieve deep, smokey tones that complement the Day of the Dead themes he favors. His relief paintings in clay—usually filled with *Muertos* images—are unique. His ceramic style influences not only his younger siblings, but his mother as well; following her son's lead, Josefina has begun to create large female figures in clay, depicting in the folds of their skirts a life story or a Oaxacan tale.

Guillermina Aguilar's children have also begun to receive recognition for their wonderful ceramics. Clay has always been a warm family-centered enterprise in this home, and Juan's churches, Alejandro's and Isabel's Virgins, Fidel's Last Suppers, Guadalupe's and Polo's Fridas, and Silvia's mermaids all reflect skill and imagination. Perhaps most interesting are the ceramic pieces of son Julian, who is thirty-one. His lyrical depiction of Saint Michael won a major award in last year's state ceramic competition in Oaxaca. And his naughty "women of the night" (an image gleaned, he says, from watching bikini-clad tourists romp on a Mexican beach) exhibit a wonderful combination of naivete and impish sexuality.

opposite left:
Bowl
Rosa García de Regino,
Dolores's daughter-in-law

opposite right:
Platter
Aurelia Regino de Guerrero,
Dolores's daughter

**Demetrio García Aguilar
with his daughter,
little Josefina**

Day of the Dead Scene
Demetrio García Aguilar

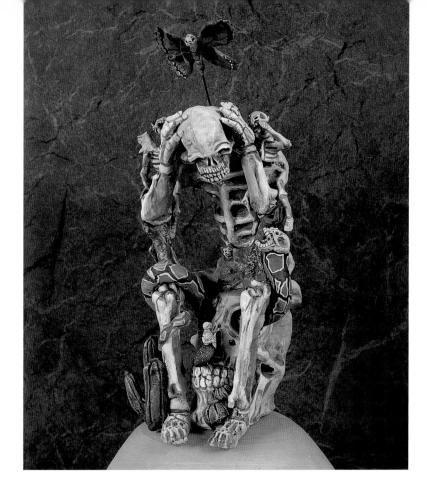

Calavera
Demetrio García Aguilar

Day of the Dead Scene
Demetrio García Aguilar

Angélica Vásquez with her parents, Delfina Cruz Díaz and Ernesto Vásquez Reyes

opposite:

Planter in the shape of a woman with lizards
Delfina Cruz Díaz and Ernesto Vásquez Reyes

The children of the other ceramists also display emerging talent. All of Dolores Porras's daughters—and daughters-in-law—have learned to create imaginative platters and vases like hers. Irene Aguilar's three children have always helped her prepare, knead, and paint her clay figures. Now sons Manuel and Juan Carlos create their own compositions with favorite Oaxacan themes such as skeletons or religious symbols. All three of Concepción Aguilar's daughters have closely watched their mother at work. Today Guadalupe Isaura, Estela, and Gabriela each recreate their own versions of their mother's designs. Like all of these devoted artisan mothers, Concepción helps in whatever way she can to further her daughters' careers, because, as she explains, "it's hard to open your own doors."

While Angélica Vásquez encourages the artistic impulse in her children, she also has urged them to continue in school. (At the moment, her youngest, fourteen-year-old Carlos, most loves to work in clay; last spring he and other young children of Oaxacan ceramists were fêted by ARIPO, the state artisan organization, with an "initiation ceremony" into the artisan life.) But instructing her parents in new ceramic techniques is now Angélica's special project: "to give them back what they once did for me, the best inheritance, teaching me to work in clay."

Her parents are skilled craftsmen, having spent their lives producing Atzompa's famed green-glazed cookware, and Angélica now helps them create more elaborate artisan designs. She counsels them on new styles and teaches them new techniques, such as how to suggest movement in clay. Her parents' fanciful new planters are very popular, and their daughter takes particular pride and joy in their success: "It's wonderful. They are rediscovering life." For the first time her mother, at sixty-six, has the money to buy a sewing machine, and her father, in his mid-seventies, is finally getting his bike. (Both are also realizing the lifelong dream of getting their teeth fixed!) Angélica laughs with pleasure, recalling her parents' childlike delight in their new achievements and possessions. But she savors too the deep satisfaction of her own role in their good fortune: "I owe them everything. How can you repay that? That doesn't have a price."

Conclusion

The folk art of the Mexican people offers a continuing testimony to the depths of creativity and imagination rooted in Mexican culture. For these six women artisans, their artistry in clay has been a vital means of self-expression, and an avenue through which they have been able to experience success, and even triumph, in their lives. They are masters at infusing into the medium of clay inordinate amounts of joy and vitality, grace and fluidity, strength and originality.

Their glorious ceramics have also provided an important means of economic survival in the harsh world of Oaxacan poverty. If these women's lives revolve around abundant talent and artistic achievement, they also reflect immoderate amounts of daily struggle and adversity. Yet their struggles are not sagas of uncommon heroism: They reflect the ordinary stories of hardship experienced, particularly by women, on a daily basis in rural Mexico.

The lives of all six ceramists have changed dramatically since their childhoods. Gone is the numbing poverty and the fear of not having enough to eat. They have all come to maturity during a time of rapid change in Mexico, when roads, electricity, and schools have penetrated even the countryside—important symbols of Mexico's impressive twentieth-century growth. Their lives show striking material change: blenders and television sets are now necessities; washing machines and electric ovens almost so.

These conveniences certainly make things easier, but these women still do not have easy lives. They reside in one of the poorest states in the country, which barely reflects the progress that has taken place in the rest of Mexico. Oaxaca continues to lag behind most other states on almost every economic or social indicator. There are also the larger crises with which they must contend. Mexico's peso crisis and global economic unrest have resulted in rising costs for firewood, paint, and clay. The worries and insecurities that plague artisan lives continue.

But the real change in these women's lives comes not from machines or roads or even the electric lights they now take for granted. They have authored the transformations in their own lives by dint of sheer talent, hard work, and grit. All six have plucked accomplishment from adversity and have dismantled, with each new ceramic piece, the enormous barriers placed in their paths as poor Oaxacan women. Their resilience is mirrored in, and sustained by, their art. Despite their struggles, they mold exuberance and jubilation out of clay. Their ceramics offer up their own joyful and inspiring celebration of life.

opposite:
Devil with Creatures
Concepción Aguilar

Glossary of Ceramic Terms and Themes

Apaxtle
Guillermina Aguilar

apaxtle. Utilitarian clay bowl—round, flat-bottomed, and with low sides—often used by potters as a water basin for moistening hands and clay.

árbol de la vida. "Tree of life." A very popular image in Mexican folk art depicting the interconnectedness of the life cycle. In Oaxcan ceramics, the imagery usually has biblical roots, employing, for example, Adam and Eve as the base figures.

arte popular. "Popular art." The art that emerges from Mexican popular culture; often a synonym for Mexican folk art.

azotador. A distinctive mallet made of baked clay; used by some ceramists to pound the clay flat.

barro áspero. "Rough clay." The mixture of clay used in Santa María Atzompa for large vessels and cooking pots.

barro de golpear. "Hitting clay" or "pounding clay." The coarse gravel-like temper used in Atzompa. It is pulverized, then mixed with "smooth clay" to produce the stronger mixture called "rough clay."

barro liso. "Smooth clay." The clay used in Atzompa for molding intricate, delicate, or decorative motifs.

bodega. Storage room used by potters for finished ware. It usually serves as the display or shop area in their homes where prospective clients view the work.

bordado. The "embroidery" style of decorating clay popularized by famed potter Teodora Blanco of Atzompa, who used elaborate clay motifs modeled in high relief on her figurines or pots.

Bordado
Dolores Porras

brasero. "Incense burner." A traditional shallow clay bowl on tripod legs used on altars, especially for Day of the Dead.

calavera. "Skull." Commonly refers to the popular skull-and-skeleton imagery used in Mexican popular art, especially for celebrating Day of the Dead.

la Catrina. The fashionably dressed skeleton figure popularized by turn-of-the-century engraver José Guadalupe Posada; now a widely used image in Mexican folk art associated with Day of the Dead.

cazuela. Ceramic casserole used extensively in home kitchens.

cempasúchil.   Traditional flower of the dead. A bright yellow-orange marigold used for Day of the Dead. Various spellings include *cempazuchitl*, *cempoalxochitl*, *zempasúchitl*.

comal.   Clay griddle used for making tortillas. In pottery-making, it often refers to the round clay covers (or broken pieces of them) piled on top of the kiln to retain heat during firing.

corriente.   "Common" or "ordinary." Refers to pottery ware made for everyday use at home, as distinct from more elaborate artisan work.

cuero.   "Hide" or "leather." Refers to the small piece of material used by ceramists to smooth and shape the clay; although still referred to as "hide," it is more common today to use felt cut from a man's hat.

chinas oaxaqueñas.   Traditionally dressed female dancers who accompany festival processions and perform at regional celebrations.

damas de la noche.   "Women of the night." A popular image for ceramics in the valley of Oaxaca inspired, according to the artisans who use it, by the scanty beach dress of American tourists and the provocative pictures of women displayed in magazines.

Día de los Angelitos.   "The Day of the Little Angels." Refers to the souls of dead children, which are believed to return on November 1, the first day of celebration honoring the dead; sweets and toys are set out for them on low altars.

Día de los Muertos.   "The Day of the Dead." The special Mexican ritual commemorating the souls of the dead, observed every November 1 and November 2 (the Roman Catholic All Saints' Day and All Souls' Day).

florero.   Clay flower vase.

Guelaguetza.   July festival in Oaxaca, also known as *Lunes del Cerro*, Monday on the Hill. On the last two Mondays in July, dancers from the seven regions of the state come together to dance for each other in traditional costumes. More generally, *guelaguetza*, the Zapotec word for "help" or "gift," symbolizes the ritual of reciprocity, or mutual exchange, so important in Oaxacan culture.

horno.   "Oven" or "kiln."

jardinera.   Clay flower pot or planter, with one flat side for hanging on a wall.

jarro.   "Clay jug." Atzompa is known for the special jug with an elongated neck and high handle its potters make that is used for hot chocolate.

Las Catrinas
Josefina Aguilar

Juego
Funeral
Irene Aguilar

Irene Aguilar inside a
mono de calenda made
by her husband

Muertos
Irene Aguilar

juego.   "Set." In Oaxaca, refers to the multi-figured scenes of Mexican ritual and daily life—baptisms, weddings, funerals—depicted in clay.

juguete.   "Toy." Also refers to the clay miniatures of pottery, tiny animals, and whistles made in Atzompa.

la Llorona.   "The Weeping Woman," a popular Mexican folktale of the tragic woman who kills her own children and is doomed to wander forever in search of them.

longas.   Thick, long ropes of clay used to build up the sides of vessels in Atzompa. Often each pottery community has its own distinct name for these clay strips.

loza verde.   Green-glazed ceramic ware for which Atzompa is renowned.

Lunes del Cerro.   See **Guelaguetza**.

maceta.   Clay flower pot or planter.

la Matlacihua.   Legend of a seductive beauty who transforms into a demon to punish men who have mistreated women; especially popular in the valley of Oaxaca. Also spelled *la Matlacihuatl.*

molde.   In Atzompa, a thick, flat disk made of baked clay on which fresh clay is shaped. Often used in other pottery communities with local variation in both shape and name.

mono de calenda.   Giant dancing puppet of a human figure or animal, usually made of papier-mâché. Used in religious festivals especially and also in the procession that takes place days before to announce the coming celebration.

Muertos.   Shorthand reference to *Día de los Muertos; muertos* literally refers to the deceased.

muñeca.   "Doll." Refers to the large unglazed clay female figures laden with elaborate clay "embroidery" popularized by Teodora Blanco of Atzompa. More generally refers to any very large ceramic female form.

músico.   "Musician." Refers to the ceramic animal figures playing musical instruments originally created by Teodora Blanco; a popular form made by many artisans in Atzompa.

nahual.   Animal spirit with the power to either protect or do harm to humans. Often referred to as *nagual* in other regions of Mexico. The theme of magical animals provides an important source of imagery in Mexican folk art.

Navidad. "Christmas."

olla. Spherical ceramic pot with a wide mouth.

rebozo. Long, rectangular multipurpose shawl worn especially by rural Mexican women.

Santo Domingo de Guzmán. Patron saint of Ocotlán de Morelos. The weeklong celebration in August to honor him is one of the most important in the community's celebratory calendar.

Semana Santa. "Holy Week." The week between Palm Sunday and Easter.

sirena. "Mermaid." An important motif in popular art throughout Mexico.

Tepeyac. The site of the miraculous appearance of the Virgin of Guadalupe; the same site where a temple to the Aztec goddess Tonantzin had stood.

Virgen de Guadalupe. "The Virgin of Guadalupe." The patron saint of Mexico. The dark-skinned Virgin announced her appearance to the poor Indian, Juan Diego, on the Hill of Tepeyac in 1531. Mexico's first saint.

Virgen de Juquila. "The Virgin of Juquila." Revered for her miraculous powers, especially in Oaxaca. Distinguished by her tiny stature, the Virgin was found in Santa Catarina Juquila, in the mountains of Oaxaca. When the temple built in her honor was destroyed by fire, the Virgin was left intact, increasing belief in her special powers. An important pilgrimage destination.

Virgen de la Asunción. "The Virgin of the Assumption." The patron saint of Santa María Atzompa, she is celebrated each August with a week of ritual, dance, and fireworks.

Virgen de la Soledad. "The Virgin of Solitude." The patroness of the capital city of Oaxaca de Juárez. An important image in Oaxacan popular art, her distinctive dress of black velvet is richly embroidered with gold and silver.

volteador. A baked clay base, typically spherical in shape, on which a *molde* is balanced and rotated. Used for making pots and large vessels in Atzompa and elsewhere. In Ocotlán, the clay base to support the distinctive rounded *molde* with handle used there for making *apaxtles* is called the *asiento* — the "seat."

Olla
Dolores Porras

following page:
**The Enchantment
of My Land**
Angélica Vásquez

Sirena
Mermaid
Angélica Vásquez